Slim and Healthy
Vegetarian

Slim and Healthy Vegetarian

JUDITH WILLS

Photography by Debbie Patterson

conran
OCTOPUS

To Tony

Throughout the book recipes are for four people unless otherwise stated. Both metric and imperial quantities are given. Use either all metric or all imperial, as the two are not necessarily interchangeable.

The publishers would like to thank Michael Gilbert & Raymond, Madame Renée Mason and the inhabitants of Couddes in France's Loire Valley for their help in the location photography.

Editorial Direction Lewis Esson Publishing
Art Direction Mary Evans
Design Alison Fenton
Design Assistant Ian Muggeridge
Photography and Styling Debbie Patterson
Illustrations Lynne Robinson
Food Styling Jane Suthering
Editorial Assistant Penny David
Production Sonya Sibbons

First published in 1994 by Conran Octopus Limited
37 Shelton Street, London WC2H 9HN

This paperback edition published in 1996 by Conran Octopus Limited
Reprinted 1997

Cataloguing in Publication Data: a catalogue record for this book is available from the British Library

ISBN 1 85029 729 0

Typesetting by Ian Muggeridge, London
Printed and bound in Singapore

CONTENTS

Vegetarian eating for health

Here we look at the constituents of a vegetarian diet and discover just why well-balanced vegetarian eating can be so healthy.

Doesn't it seem such a very long time ago that vegetarians were thought of as a cranky minority to be viewed with suspicion and offered – *always* – cheese omelette if we ever inadvertently let one near our supper tables?

Today, even if we're not vegetarian – or demi-vegetarian – ourselves, we almost all have at least one vegetarian in the family and we all have several vegetarian friends. It is estimated that there are currently about three million people in this country who don't eat meat and the number is growing day by day.

There is also a growing number of vegetarian cookbooks on the shelves. Sadly, many of them are still caught in the trap of too much *worthiness* and too little variety and taste. Others don't do vegetarianism any favour by including far too many recipes stuffed full of fats, oils and high-fat dairy products. Surely one of the main reasons that people today turn to vegetarian eating is that it is – or should be – a *healthy* way to eat, as well as a kind and compassionate one?

So it is for people who are still seeking healthy yet tasty, light yet satisfying, wide-ranging yet simple – and above all easy, or fairly easy and quick-to-prepare – meals that I have researched *Slim and Healthy Vegetarian*.

Within these pages I hope that you will find a collection of meals to suit you and your lifestyle as well as your body. I hope also that you will appreciate the first two chapters containing all the basic information the new vegetarian (or part-time vegetarian) needs to ensure a balanced, appealing diet.

You will also, I hope, be pleased to see – as you flick through the menus and recipes – that, within the limits of vegetarianism itself, there are no 'banned' foods at all. Certain high-fat, low-nutrient foods may be limited, for sure, but you will see you can incorporate fabulous cakes, cookies, desserts and pastries into a healthy diet, as well as cheeses, cream and oils.

The secret of any good diet is balance and taste. That is what *Slim and Healthy Vegetarian* is all about. Enjoy it – and remember that enjoyment is twice as sweet when there is no guilt attached!

WHAT IS A VEGETARIAN?

There are several different 'degrees' of vegetarianism and, if you are new to the subject or are unsure about catering for a vegetarian, it is important to clarify the differences straight away. In fact, if you are cooking for any vegetarian it is always a good idea to ask them *exactly* what they don't eat to avoid any embarrassment at serving time.

DEMI-VEGETARIANS aren't true vegetarians, but I include a description here as many people who call themselves 'vegetarians' are, in fact, 'demis'. Normally, demi-vegetarians can be described as people who don't eat any red meat, but will eat poultry and fish from time to time. However, some demi-vegetarians eat no poultry either, just fish.

Also, some people who call themselves demi-vegetarians *do* eat red meat occasionally – they will, say, eat it if there is nothing else on offer at a dinner party but would not eat it at home. So if someone says they are 'demi-veg', it is important to enquire further!

VEGETARIANS can be divided into two sub-groups:

Lacto-ovo-vegetarians eat no flesh of any kind – no meat, poultry or fish. They *do* eat eggs and all dairy produce, including cheese, milk, yogurt and butter.

Lacto-vegetarians eat everything lacto-ovo-vegetarians eat except eggs.

So, again – when catering for vegetarians it is important to know whether they will or won't eat eggs.

VEGANS go further than vegetarians, eating no flesh, no eggs and no dairy produce of any kind. Some vegans will eat honey, others won't. Some avoid any connection with what they consider cruelty to animals by not wearing leather or fur, and not using cosmetics or other products tested on animals. They eat nothing but plant foods.

FRUITARIANS are even stricter than vegans, eating only fruits, nuts and seeds. The fruitarian diet is very restricted and beyond the scope of this book.

Apart from fruitarians, all other types of true vegetarian will find recipes to suit them in the following chapters,
– although, as most vegetarians are lacto-ovo-vegetarians, the majority of recipes are more suitable for them.

If you are vegetarian – or thinking of going vegetarian – it is up to you to decide what you will and won't eat – and why. Many people give up eating flesh on moral or compassionate grounds, but perhaps the biggest reason people make the change to vegetarianism is that they hope it will improve their health and well-being – and perhaps it will help to keep them slim.

HOW HEALTHY IS A VEGETARIAN DIET?

Indeed, if you follow a well-balanced vegetarian diet, all the research to date appears to confirm that you will be eating healthily. Here's why:

★ It should be lower in saturated fats (found mainly in meat and dairy produce) and in fats in general than an average carnivorous diet – particularly veganism.

★ It should be high in complex carbohydrates. These are the unrefined or low-refined starchy foods that should form the majority of the average vegetarian diet – bread, rice and other grains, pasta, potatoes, cereals, dried beans, peas and lentils and fresh fruits and vegetables. These complex carbohydrates provide bulk for the diet, plenty of fibre and most also provide good amounts of protein. This makes for a diet high in benefits, including less risk of heart disease and certain forms of cancer, less digestive disorders, obesity and diabetes. (Oats and pulses in particular appear to have an especially beneficial effect on blood cholesterol levels.)

★ It should be high in vitamins, especially the antioxidant vitamins beta-carotene, C and E. Beta-carotene is a 'proform' of vitamin A (ie the body converts it to vitamin A) and it is found in many brightly coloured vegetables and fruits. These anti-oxidant vitamins appear to offer protection against heart disease and cancers. Optimum vitamin intake also has many other health benefits.

★ It should be low in refined products and products high in additives.

★ It should help us to stay slim. A reduced-fat diet, high in complex carbohydrates, naturally limits overall calorie intake by helping us to feel full both during and after eating and by providing plenty of 'bulk' on the plate.

No wonder, then, that vegetarians have:

★ On average, a 20% lower blood cholesterol level than meat eaters.

★ A 30% lower cancer rate than meat eaters.

★ Less incidence than meat eaters of all the following: heart disease, kidney stones, osteoporosis, diabetes, diverticulitis, piles, angina, gout, dental decay and rheumatoid arthritis.

The fact is that a well-balanced vegetarian diet consisting of a high proportion of fresh fruit and vegetables and starchy foods is almost the exact recipe for healthy eating as prescribed by the World Health Organization (WHO) in 1990 and Britain's COMA committee in 1991.

GETTING IT RIGHT

However, not everyone who goes vegetarian does eat such a well-balanced diet, low in fat and high in complex carbohydrates and vitamins. Here are some ways in which a vegetarian diet may not be as healthy as it could be:

★ Some people just give up meat, poultry and fish and simply carry on eating the rest of their diet as before – eg a roast meal with roast potatoes and vegetables but no meat, or fish and chips without the fish! Such a diet is likely to be short of both protein and calories, and is likely to make the new vegetarian hungry and quickly bored with 'vegetarian' eating.

★ Some people give up flesh and simply replace it by eating extra cheese and eggs. There is nothing wrong with cheese and eggs in small amounts – especially low-fat cheese, but many types of cheese contain a great deal of saturated fat. Traditional Cheddar, for example, contains three-quarters of its calories as fat calories, even eggs are 67% fat and only 33% protein, and in 100 calories' worth of whole milk 52 of them are fat calories! So just by giving up meat, poultry and fish, it doesn't necessarily mean vegetarians will be cutting down on fat if instead they choose high-fat dairy produce as protein sources.

★ Many vegetarians carry on eating a high-fat diet because they eat a lot of butter or margarine on bread, or oil in cooking. They often eat a lot of pastry – most of which is very high in fat – and baked goods. Many also eat lots of fat in the form of cakes, desserts, biscuits and confectionery – perhaps thinking that, because they are cutting down on animal produce, they don't need to feel guilty about indulging their sweet tooth.

★ People who are vegan may also have problems – if they are not careful, they may fall short on various nutrients, particularly iron, protein, calcium and vitamin B12.

However, all these potential problems are not difficult to overcome with a little know-how. There is no need to turn yourself into a walking nutrition manual, though. All you need is a little time to learn the basics, and then you can easily build a balanced and pleasant vegetarian diet.

THE NUTRIENTS WE NEED

All the food that we eat provides us with calories (ie, energy). The calories in our food can be calories from carbohydrate, calories from fat or calories from protein. If we get the right balance of those three energy-giving foods, we should also get a good balance of the other things we need for good health – vitamins, minerals, trace elements and fibre. (Of course, it goes without saying that we also need water.)

An average female diet to maintain a reasonable body weight contains about 2,000 calories a day; for men the figure is around 2,700. For optimum health, according to World Health Organization recommendations, we should aim to eat no more than 30% of those calories as fat, we should eat at least 55% of those calories as carbohydrate, and 10–15% of them as protein.

For practical purposes, there is no such thing as a food that is purely carbohydrate (except sugar) or purely fat (except oil) or purely protein – most are a mix of at least two of those elements. Nevertheless, foods can be grouped as predominantly carbohydrate foods and predominantly fat foods. The best protein sources in a vegetarian diet tend to be from low-fat, high-carbohydrate foods. Very few vegetarian foods are predominantly protein.

CARBOHYDRATES

These are the starchy and sugary foods.

The complex carbohydrates as mentioned above are the unrefined plant foods of all types. We include all fruits and vegetables in this group because, although many fruits and vegetables are quite low in starch, they add bulk and fibre to the diet. All of these complex carbohydrates – with the exception of most fruits – also contain good or very good amounts of low-fat protein.

Pulses – all dried peas, beans and lentils – deserve a special mention because not only are they a very low-fat food, they also contain more protein than the other complex carbohydrate foods – around 30%.

Fruits and vegetables are an important part of your diet because, as well as providing lots of bulk, fibre and colour to your plate for few calories, they are also one of the vegetarian's most important sources of vitamins and minerals.

The sugary or 'simple' carbohydrates are sugars, syrups, honey, glucose – these types of carbohydrates contain no fibre and few if any vitamins and minerals. According to the WHO, they should form no more than 10% of your total calorie intake (within the 55% already mentioned for total carbohydrate intake).

So, obviously, as complex carbohydrate calories should make up around half of your daily diet, it is important that you include several from this group in your diet each day and at each meal.

FATS
There are three types of fat in our diet: saturated, monounsaturated and polyunsaturated.

Saturated fat is the type mostly found in red meat and dairy produce. Because of the apparent link between a high saturated fat diet and heart disease, some cancers, obesity and other health problems, the WHO suggests that we should limit our saturated fat intake to 10% of total calories and a third of total fat intake. That is why it is important on a vegetarian diet not to rely too heavily on dairy produce for your protein unless it is mostly low-fat dairy produce.

Most fatty foods contain at least some monounsaturated fats, but both olive oil and groundnut oil are particularly high in them. Monounsaturated fat is not linked with heart disease and it could, indeed, have a beneficial effect on the cardio-vascular system. Around 10% of your day's total calories could come from this type of monounsaturated fat.

Polyunsaturated fats are, again, present to some degree in most fatty foods, but found in largest quantities in sunflower, corn, rape seed and safflower oils. Polyunsaturates can reduce blood cholesterol levels and we should aim to consume, again, 10% of our daily calories as polyunsaturates – bringing our total daily fat intake to 30%. Less fat than this certainly wouldn't do us any harm – especially those trying to lose weight.

A diet high in plant foods will naturally ensure that the balance of the three types of fat is kept at a reasonable level. So as long as you take care not to consume too much of the high-fat vegetarian foods you shouldn't have a problem with too much fat in your diet.

HIGH-FAT VEGETARIAN FOODS TO EAT IN SMALL OR MODERATE AMOUNTS:

* All cheeses, except those specifically marked 'low-fat' (even half-fat cheeses do contain quite a lot of fat).
* Whole milk – choose semi-skimmed or skimmed, or soya milk instead.
* Cream, all kinds – choose non-dairy lower-fat cream substitute instead (eg 'Shape Single') or yogurt.
* Butter – choose low-fat spread instead.
* Eggs: although a good source of protein and vitamins, consumption is best restricted to three or four a week.
* Nuts: all nuts, except chestnuts, are very high in fat, with moderate amounts of protein, so if you are watching your weight they are best used in small quantities within other dishes or as a special treat.
* Seeds: as nuts.
* Coconut flesh and cream: high in saturated fat, use with caution!
* Pastry – choose filo instead, which allows you to control the amount and type of fat that you brush on it.
* Desserts, sweets and baked goods: experiment with lower-fat, lower-sugar recipes, such as the ones on pages 106–17. Grated carrot or sweet potato or mashed banana can all be added to bakes to give bulk, 'mouth feel', texture and sweetness rather than using lots of fat and sugar.
* Cooking oils and salad oils: just go easy on these – most recipes use far more oil than is necessary.

Experiment to see how much you can cut down, as I have done in the recipes in this book. Add flavour with calorie-free herbs and spices.

PROTEIN
Protein is the material with which we build and repair new body tissue. Adults need around 10–15% of their daily calories to be protein and, in fact, most meat-eaters get much more than this.

New vegetarians often worry about whether or not they will get enough protein in their diet – especially if they don't want to eat too much dairy produce (traditionally a good source of protein after flesh foods). As protein is contained in such a wide range of plant foods, however, if you get a varied diet containing enough calories overall it is highly unlikely that you would suffer a protein shortage, even if you eat no dairy produce at all.

Why then, for so long, was vegetable protein thought of as 'second class' protein? Well, protein is made up of

20 different amino acids. Eight of these amino acids are called 'essential', because the body can't synthesize them itself and so they must be provided in our food. Meat and animal products contain these eight essential amino acids in one 'package', whereas most vegetable sources of protein contain some, but not all. For example, lentils are high in the amino acid lysine, while rice is low in lysine but higher in the other seven. So if you eat, say, rice and lentils at the same meal, you will be getting a 'complete' protein meal with everything you need supplied by the two different plant products.

Until recently it was thought that for vegetarians to obtain enough 'complete' protein from their diet, they would have to combine the different types of plant protein at each meal. The newest thinking says that as long as you have a varied and well-balanced diet on a daily basis, it isn't absolutely essential always to eat 'complementary' proteins at each meal.

However, as the complementary proteins theory is really quite simple, it is worth listing the combinations of plant foods here that *will* give you complete protein within one meal:

1 Grains (rice, rye, wheat, barley, millet, corn, buckwheat, etc) with a pulse (lentils, beans of any kind, peas). Some examples: beans on toast, rice and bean salad, hummus with pitta, lentil pâté with crispbread, split pea soup with rolls.
2 Pulses with nuts or seeds. Some examples: chickpea and sesame seed salad, cashew dip with crudités followed by lentil soup.
3 Any plant protein with milk, milk products and eggs. This means the protein quality of any plant food can be enhanced by the addition of a little low-fat dairy produce. Some examples: potatoes contain good amounts of protein which can be made complete with the addition of a low-fat cheese sauce; rice can be enhanced by adding skimmed milk for a rice pudding.

As you can see, most of the time we practise this 'protein complementing' without even thinking about it, because the combinations of foods seem natural.

All the main meal, supper and main course salad recipes in this book will give you 'complete protein' – and, if you add bread of some kind to your soups, dips, spreads and starters, you will also get complete protein from most of them.

However, do remember that as long as you get a good variety of food on a daily basis, you don't really need to worry too much about this protein combining, and most plant foods – with the exception of fruit – contain good amounts of protein. Incidentally, soya beans in all their forms are the best source of low-fat protein.

Here are some other good sources:
* Soya flour, tofu, textured vegetable protein (TVP), myco-protein ('Quorn'), chickpeas, lentils, beans of all kinds, split peas, brown rice, rye, oatmeal, wheat and wheatgerm, millet, corn, barley, pasta, potatoes.
* Nuts and seeds are a good source, but have a high fat content (around 70%) and so are high in calories.
* Leafy green vegetables also contain good amounts of protein though, as they are high-bulk low-calorie foods, it would be hard to get enough protein from them alone.

VITAMINS, MINERALS AND FIBRE

Vegetarians who get adequate calories and complex carbohydrates, fruit and vegetables are highly unlikely to need to worry about whether or not they are getting adequate vitamins and minerals in their diet.

All foods – apart from simple sugars – contain trace elements, and all plant food contains fibre. The proportions and amounts vary from food to food – for instance, oranges are a good source of vitamin C but contain low amounts of most of the B vitamins; while peanuts are a good source of vitamin E, but contain no vitamin C at all.

So, again, as long as you eat a good varied diet you should get a good cross-section of vitamins and minerals.

For interest and easy reference I have listed below the main sources in a vegetarian diet of all the most important vitamins and minerals, plus the best sources of fibre (for your guidance they are listed within each section in order of richness). Also all the recipes in the book have a nutrition panel containing vitamin and mineral information.

VITAMIN A (retinol) – important for good vision.
Best sources: all dairy produce.
BETA-CAROTENE (can be converted to vitamin A in the body) – anti-oxidant vitamin thought to offer protection against heart disease and cancers.
Best sources: carrots, parsley, red chillies, kale, spinach, dark green leaves of all kinds, sweet potatoes, apricots, nectarines, watercress, tomato purée, broccoli, vine leaves, fennel, cantaloupe melon, peaches, leeks, squash, mango, prunes, tomatoes, asparagus, peas, sweetcorn.

VITAMIN B group (consists of six different B vitamins, usually grouped together because they often occur in the same type of food) – important mainly for maintaining a healthy nervous system and converting food into energy.

VITAMIN B1 (thiamine)

Best sources: brewers' yeast, sunflower seeds, millet, yeast extract, wheatgerm, coriander leaves, soya beans, alfalfa sprouts, Brazil nuts, whole-wheat spaghetti, peanuts, sesame seeds, adzuki beans, split peas, millet, rolled oats, black-eye beans, kidney beans, chickpeas, lentils, other nuts and pulses.

VITAMIN B2 (riboflavin)

Best sources: yeast extract, brewers' yeast, Chinese mushrooms, almonds, wheatgerm, Camembert and Danish Blue cheeses, alfalfa, egg yolk, adzuki beans, Cheddar, Parmesan and Edam cheeses, mushrooms, soya beans, broccoli, yogurt, black-eye beans, other nuts and pulses.

VITAMIN B3 (niacin)

Best sources: yeast extract, brewers' yeast, peanuts, Chinese mushrooms, soya beans, wholemeal spaghetti, wheatgerm, Parmesan cheese, barley, black-eye beans, brown rice, split peas, wheat, lentils, butter beans, wholemeal bread.

VITAMIN B6 (pyridoxine)

Best sources: wheatgerm, soya beans, oats, walnuts, lentils, butter beans, haricots, barley, hazelnuts, bananas, mung beans, peanuts, kidney beans, avocados, white rice, sultanas, Brussels sprouts, kale, leeks, potatoes, prunes, sweet potato, broccoli, red cabbage, Camembert cheese.

VITAMIN B12 (cobalamin)

Best sources: egg yolk, hard and cottage cheeses, yeast extract, milk, fortified soya milk, seaweed.

IMPORTANT NOTE: Vegans should take special care to get enough vitamin B12 in their diets.

FOLIC ACID

Best sources: yeast extract, black-eye beans, wheatgerm, endive, brewers' yeast, chickpeas, mung beans, broccoli, kidney beans, spinach, Brussels sprouts, butter beans, peanuts, spring greens, okra, soya beans, almonds, beetroot, cabbage, Chinese leaves, peas, hazelnuts, parsnips, avocado, walnuts, Camembert, oatmeal, runner beans, sweet potato, corn, other whole grains and pulses.

VITAMIN C (ascorbic acid) – important for healthy tissues and the absorption of minerals: the antioxidant vitamin. Heat and light will destroy.

Best sources: guavas, green chillies, red peppers, blackcurrants, parsley, kale, sorrel, broccoli, green peppers, tomato purée, red chillies, Brussels sprouts, lemons, cauliflower, cabbage, strawberries, watercress, red cabbage, spinach, oranges, limes, gooseberries, grapefruit, lychees, mango, beansprouts, new potatoes, spring greens, tangerines, melon, okra, peas, pineapple, raspberries, swede, sweet potato, all other fresh fruit and vegetables.

VITAMIN D (cholecalciferol) – important for the body's absorption of calcium.

Best sources: can be manufactured by the body in sunlight, otherwise found in fortified margarines and dairy produce.

VITAMIN E (tocopherols) – important for healthy skin and cells and also an important antioxidant.

Best sources: wheatgerm oil, sunflower oil, safflower oil, palm oil, sunflower margarines, wheatgerm, hazelnuts, almonds, pecans, rape seed oil, peanut oil, corn oil, soya oil, peanuts, green cabbage, Brazil nuts, olive oil, sweet potatoes, avocados, asparagus, butter, spinach, oatmeal, eggs, wholemeal flour, broccoli, tomatoes, spring greens, Brussels sprouts, blackcurrants, Parmesan cheese, barley, soya beans, brown rice.

IRON – needed for healthy blood; absorption improved by eating vitamin C at same meal.

Best sources: dulse (seaweed), curry powder, pistachios, alfalfa, Chinese mushrooms, adzuki beans, wheatgerm, soya beans, mung beans, sesame seeds, lentils, soya flour, dried peaches and apricots, millet, haricot beans, black-eye beans, chickpeas, egg yolk, barley, butter beans, split peas, tofu, bulghar, pasta verdi, soya sauce, Brazil nuts, broad beans, oatmeal, wholemeal flour, cashew nuts, white pasta, wholemeal bread.

CALCIUM – needed for healthy bones and teeth and correct functioning of cardiovascular system.

Best sources: seaweed, Parmesan, Cheddar and Edam, molasses, tofu, vine leaves, Feta and Camembert cheeses, dried figs, almonds, kale, soya beans, Brazil nuts, yogurt, haricot beans, Chinese leaves, chickpeas, kidney beans, sesame seeds, egg yolk, milk, muesli, black-eye beans, broad beans, broccoli, mung beans, rhubarb, low-fat soft cheeses, currants, spinach, dried apricots, spring greens, butter beans, adzuki beans, Chinese mushrooms, okra.

ZINC – needed for the correct functioning of the healing processes and enzyme activity.

Best sources: wheatgerm, sesame seeds, yeast, alfalfa, sunflower seeds, oats, Brazil nuts, curry powder, Cheddar, Edam and Parmesan cheeses, split peas, adzuki beans, egg yolk, barley, almonds, lentils, Camembert cheese, walnuts, peanuts, rye, wholemeal flour, wholemeal bread, other pulses.

POTASSIUM – needed for cellular activity.

Best sources: seaweed, molasses, dried apricots, butter beans, soya beans, soya flour, haricot beans, dates, currants, peanut butter, walnuts, black-eye beans, lentils, potatoes, barley, mushrooms, spinach, coconut, corn on the cob, pasta, rye, avocados, banana, sweet potato.

FIBRE

Best sources: dried apricots, dried figs, prunes, dried peaches, almonds, soya and wholewheat flour, dried beans of all kind, lentils of all kinds, split peas, chickpeas, oatmeal, raspberries.

Notes: Raw wheat bran is high in fibre but shouldn't be relied upon as a regular fibre source as it can prevent the body absorbing certain minerals which are eaten at the same time.

All the other trace elements not mentioned here will be supplied in a diet rich in the above vitamins.

GOING VEGETARIAN?

In the next two chapters you will get plenty of advice and practical tips on stocking up your larder and on menu planning, but if you are still simply thinking of going vegetarian the best advice both for practical purposes and for bodily acclimatization is to do so gradually.

People who come off a typical Western high-fat, low-fibre diet on to suddenly large amounts of lentils, beans, vegetables and grains often find their digestive systems protesting – hardly surprising. The same would be true of a vegetarian suddenly giving up their diet and going on a high-meat, low-fibre diet!

So give your body a chance to adapt and give yourself a chance to get used to different ways of shopping, meal planning and cooking by making the process of conversion a gradual one.

Here are some ways you could make the gradual change:

1   Replace meat, poultry and fish meals twice a week for two weeks. Then increase this to three times a week for two weeks, and so on, until you have eliminated flesh altogether. Meanwhile, busy yourself building up a collection of meals that you enjoy.

2   Cut down portion sizes of flesh products on your plate and increase portion sizes of plant foods. Aim to replace the flesh products with the high-protein plant foods such as pulses and try not to rely too much on dairy produce.

The easiest way to alter the balance on your plate is to create 'composite' dishes – eg pilaffs, risotti, curries, paellas, mixed salads, stir-fries, etc. You can also, if you like, use vegetable protein (eg soya mince or chunks of 'Quorn' mince or chunks of 'VegeMince') as a meat substitute until you get more used to basic vegetarian cooking.

3   First cut out red meat for a few weeks. Replace it with high-protein vegetarian foods as above, then cut out poultry for another few weeks, again replacing that with vegetarian dishes, not simply more fish. Finally, cut out fish too, replacing that with more vegetarian dishes.

A VEGETARIAN IN THE FAMILY

Shopping and cooking for a lone vegetarian can seem a daunting proposition but it isn't really. Here are some ideas to help you:

★   Enjoy eating with the vegetarian at least a couple of times a week – why cook those delicious meals if you don't enjoy them yourself at least some of the time?

★   Once or twice a week, make similar meals to those you are making for the non-vegetarians in the family, but use vegetarian protein instead – eg a cottage pie using TVP, a 'Quorn' and mushroom flan instead of chicken and mushroom, a tofu stir-fry instead of a turkey one. Whenever you are making non-vegetarian bakes, flans and so on, make an individual container with a vegetarian filling for the vegetarian – or freeze it for later.

★   Don't feel guilty about using vegetarian 'fast foods' to create quick and easy meals for one – pastas, rice, pitta breads, salads and vegetable stir-fries are all nutritious and tasty.

★   Batch-cook and freeze a selection of the soups, sauces and dips from the appropriate chapters in this book. You can then easily create instant meals. (For more advice, read the 'Short Cuts to Good Food' section on page 29.)

So now let's turn all this advice on nutrition into practical reality. The next chapter will show you how to build up a really workable and interesting vegetarian store cupboard.

The vegetarian kitchen

Planning a delicious and nutritious vegetarian diet is made much easier with the help of a well-stocked larder. Here you'll find all the information you will need about buying, storing and preparing every type of vegetarian food.

Every vegetarian cook should aim to build up a comprehensive larder of basic – and more exotic – items. You'll then find that, with the addition of a very few fresh ingredients or side dishes, you'll never be at a loss for a quick and easy – or even a more elaborate – meal.

This chapter guides you through the contents of the ideal store cupboard, fridge and freezer; with tips on buying, storing, shelf-life and preparation. If you're a new vegetarian, starting to cook for a vegetarian, or perhaps a long-term vegetarian who has slipped into lazy ways, you'll find the information here invaluable. Having a well-stocked larder will help you to avoid the trap that so many vegetarians fall into – boring, monotonous meals and incomplete nutrition. However busy or inexperienced you are, you needn't resign yourself to that. In fact I've devoted a special section to the busy cook (and who isn't busy these days, at least some of the time?). You'll see that, with a very little planning, shopping and cooking can be made quick and easy.

Once you know *what* to buy, *where* to buy is no longer a problem for vegetarians. At last, a variety of good quality items is not hard to find. Whereas no more than 10 years ago you would find it hard to obtain more than one or two different kinds of, say, dried bean at the local supermarket and hardly any more at the health-food shop, you can now easily find ten or more varieties at the supermarket alone. Supermarkets are also a good place to seek out speciality oils and vinegars, cheese, pasta and grains.

Your local health-food store is still well worth browsing around, for most have the widest selection of dried fruits, spices and nuts – also at lower cost. Your corner deli is bound to be a good source of the more exotic lines in bottles, jars and cans of speciality items, and also of unusual breads and tea breads.

Home-dried Tomatoes (page 125)

Lastly, the chapter looks at fresh fruit and vegetables, with a guide to the more exotic varieties and important advice on buying and storing. The recent wide availability of good vegetarian foodstuffs is all thanks to the growing demand from the ever-increasing army of vegetarians, part-time vegetarians and demi-vegetarians. This trend is bound to continue and will do so quicker if you remember when you don't find what you're looking for to make a point of asking. Many stores will buy in specially for you.

One great bonus of vegetarian food is that most of the basics are inexpensive – so there is no need to feel at all guilty when you purchase those luxury items. Shopping for your vegetarian meals – and cooking to fill up the freezer when you have the time – are two very enjoyable pastimes, so don't be afraid to buy and don't be afraid to experiment.

GRAINS

If grains mean little more to you than long-grain rice or rolled oats, here's where your thinking starts to change! Grains of many kinds are a staple part of the vegetarian diet – and a delicious one, too! Grains are almost perfect food – high in carbohydrate, low in fat and containing good amounts of protein, vitamins and minerals – so use them as often as you can. Start off with two or three kinds and gradually try out more as you get more confident.

Store grains in airtight containers in cool dry conditions, and used within one year for whole grains or three months for rolled or flaked grains and flours.

You will find some of the grains described here in your supermarket; for others you may have to visit your health-food shop, but try to ensure it is a health-food shop with a rapid turnover so that your grains aren't likely to be stale when you buy them.

BARLEY

The kind of barley you want to buy is 'pot' barley rather than 'pearl' barley, the latter having been milled of much of its goodness. Pot barley is a good addition to soups and casseroles and can be served as a grain on its own. It does have a long cooking time, however – up to two hours!

BUCKWHEAT

High in nutrients, it is particularly popular in Russia. The grains can be boiled like rice or ground into buckwheat flour, which is particularly good mixed with equal parts of whole-wheat flour for pancakes.

BULGHAR

This is the name for wheat that has gone through a process of cracking, hulling and cooking so that it simply needs soaking to make it ready to eat or, occasionally, a little further boiling or steaming. Bulghar makes a nice change from rice and is probably best known for its use in the Mediterranean herb salad *tabbouleh*.

CORN

Also called maize. Buy some corn grains to make home-made popcorn (it's easy – just add a layer to a little oil in a heavy lidded pan and heat until you hear the popping!)

Fine cornmeal makes polenta – a delicious supper dish (see page 74) and you can also buy cornmeal to make Mexican tacos and delicious cornbread.

COUSCOUS

Yet another form of wheat, it is tiny bits of ready-cooked semolina that need only soaking to be ready to eat (it can be soaked in stock for more flavour). Widely used in North Africa, it is good with beans as a vegetable stuffing.

MILLET

This golden grain is high in iron. Try stir-frying the whole grains in a little oil, then boiling them like rice until soft.

OATS

These are particularly good at staving off hunger pangs and are rich in nutrients. Flakes are used for porridge, muesli and oatcakes (see page 114) and can also be used as a sweet or savoury topping for bakes and crumbles.

You can also use oatmeal mixed with wheat flour for a tasty bread. Use oatmeal up quickly as its high oil content means it can go rancid quite readily.

RICE

Brown rice is the whole grain and contains the most vitamin B. It takes around 40 minutes to boil and has a good nutty flavour and bite to it.

White rice comes in many varieties. There is nothing wrong with the ordinary *long-grain rice* you can buy everywhere (look at the pack to ensure you are not buying a bag containing a lot of broken rice grains – a sign of poor quality). It contains less fibre and vitamins than brown rice, but that may not matter in a varied diet. Of the long-grain white rices, my favourite is Basmati rice for good flavour and easy cooking, especially to accompany Indian dishes and in paellas. For use in Far-Eastern dishes, *Thai fragrant rice* (Jasmine rice) is better, producing a classic, softer texture. *Arborio rice* is perhaps the best-known of the Italian rices for risotto – it is shorter-grained than long-grain rice and absorbs more liquid.

Pudding rice, with its short round grains, should not be used for savoury dishes, but is more suitable for, say, baked rice puddings.

Wild rice is not really a rice at all but looks like it. It is an expensive black, or near-black, grain that can take quite a time to cook but will add flavour, colour and interest to rice dishes and salads. It is usually not served on its own, but mixed in small proportions with other rice – possibly because of its costliness.

RYE

This strong-flavoured grain can be cracked and boiled like rice; rye flour can be used with wheat flour to make a robust bread. The cooked grains can also be used in many savoury dishes.

WHEAT

The major source of carbohydrate in our Western diets.

Cracked wheat can be bought and cooked like rice. Wheat flakes can be added to muesli or crumble toppings.

Wheat flour is, of course, used for bread, cakes and pastry-making, as well as pasta (see below). It is best to use whole-grain wheat most of the time, but refined white wheat flour is a good source of calcium and you shouldn't refuse to eat it now and then!

The outer part of the wheat grain when milled is called *bran* and is high in fibre: do not, however, sprinkle it on everything as it can impede absorption of minerals. The inner part of the wheat grain is *wheatgerm*, which is a valuable addition to breakfast cereals, or may be sprinkled in drinks or on fruit or added to bread.

See also bulghar and couscous.

PASTA

You can make your own pasta even without any special equipment (see page 120), or you can buy a pasta machine and make a variety of shapes.

Pasta is basically a mixture of wheat flour (hard durum wheat is best) and water, with or without eggs. Vegans should note that bought fresh pasta usually contains eggs, whereas dried pasta usually does not.

Whole-grain pasta contains more fibre and B vitamins than white or coloured pasta; nevertheless white pasta is still a good source of carbohydrate and protein.

If you buy your pasta dried, stock up your store cupboard with three or four different kinds. Pasta keeps well

and, as you experiment, you will find that different types and shapes are best for different uses. Here are the basics to stock:

Lasagne sheets: plain, whole-wheat or verde (with spinach). For lasagne or can be rolled into cannelloni tubes.

Macaroni: good with cheese sauce or in bakes.

Shells (small): good for salads and heavy sauces.

Shells (large): good for filling with a savoury sauce and serving as a starter.

Flat pasta (eg *tagliatelle*): good with creamy sauces and pesto.

Long thin pasta (eg *spaghetti*, *spaghettini*): good with 'runny' sauces that contain no large pieces (eg tomato).

(The coloured pastas simply make the plate look nicer, especially if you have a non-colourful sauce.)

Note: all pasta should be cooked only until 'al dente', ie still with a bite.

NOODLES

Noodles are similar to pasta in many ways – a mixture of flour and water, sometimes with egg. Here are a few you may consider adding to your store cupboard, as they are so versatile and easy and quick to prepare:

Egg-thread noodles (medium or fine): used in Chinese cooking, they are ready to soak and eat: only suitable for lacto-ovo-vegetarians.

Rice noodles: thin and white and made from rice flour; suitable for vegans.

Cellophane noodles: fine transparent noodles made from mung bean flour and water; suitable for vegans.

PULSES

Pulses are all the dried beans, peas and lentils and are the major source of protein in the vegetarian diet. They all have to be soaked and boiled before eating, although you can buy most kinds pre-cooked and canned if you only want a small quantity. It is always wise to have a few cans of pulses in your store cupboard for those inevitable times when you need to make a quick soup, salad or whatever, but hadn't got round to soaking.

A soaking and boiling time chart appears overleaf, as the pulses vary enormously in their needs. There also follows a run-through of some of the various pulses you may like to stock. They are all so versatile – you eat them hot, cold, whole, puréed on bread, as a dip … and, of course,

The vegetarian kitchen

they are a low-cost item, so you needn't feel guilty about experimenting. I said grains are an almost perfect food – perhaps pulses are, for vegetarians, THE perfect food!

Buy your pulses, like your grains, from a supermarket or health store with a rapid turnover; if pulses are very old, they tend to need much longer cooking times.

BEANS

Adzuki beans: very nutritious small red beans, often used for sprouting.

Black beans: small shiny beans, good in soups and casseroles.

Black-eye beans: creamy beans with a black eye, sweet and pretty in salads as well as robust enough for soups and casseroles.

Borlotti beans: pale pinkish-brown bean from Italy, nice for salads and risotti.

Broad beans: brown if they still have skins on and white if removed; good for dips, salads and casseroles.

Butter beans: tasty and creamy served hot or cold; they go especially well with onions and tomatoes.

Cannellini beans: type of haricot bean but larger; their mild flavour is widely used in Italian cooking and they are great in salads.

Flageolet beans: pale-green variety of haricot with a delicate flavour, much used in France.

Ful medames (Egyptian brown beans): small dark-brown, richly flavoured, the national Egyptian bean, often baked there with eggs, garlic and spices.

Haricot beans: well-known variety, the original 'baked bean' (make your own beans in tomato sauce using these); they are also good in baked dishes and soups.

Kidney beans (red kidney bean): everyone knows these large red beans; ideal for colour and flavour, they are used in many dishes, are robust enough to cook well with spices and make good pâté.

Lima beans: smaller version of butter beans, with slightly sweeter flavour.

Mung beans: small and green, often used for sprouting.

Pinto beans: speckled variety of haricots found in Italy; pretty in salads.

Soya beans: a 'complete' protein, containing all of the essential amino acids – so include soya and soya products in your store cupboard. Unfortunately, however, they take ages to cook. You can add cooked beans to soups and casseroles. You can also sprout soya beans.

PEAS

Chickpeas (garbanzo beans): not really a 'pea' but a seed, it has a floury full flavour when cooked; important ingredient of Mediterranean and Indian cooking and valuable for vegetarians as a source of protein, fibre and calcium. The cooked 'peas' can be used in casseroles and bakes, in salads and puréed for dips or dhal. Also try Falafel Patties (see page 81).

Split peas: either green or yellow; quick to cook and good for soups.

Whole peas: you can also get whole ordinary green peas dried, which may be useful if you don't have much room in your freezer for frozen peas. However, dried peas don't contain as much vitamin C as fresh or frozen ones.

LENTILS

All lentils are quick to cook, versatile, delicious and good sources of low-fat protein. They can also be sprouted.

Brown lentils: you can buy very small whole brown lentils, which are very flavourful, or slightly larger Continental brown lentils, again with a great robust flavour but often cooking up slightly softer than the smaller version.

Green lentils: similar to the large brown ones, but a sludgy green colour and slightly less flavourful.

Puy lentils: these French lentils are sometimes called the 'gourmet's lentils' because they have a better flavour and are harder to obtain – and thus more expensive – than ordinary small brown lentils, which they resemble although they are slightly greyer. They are good in all lentil recipes.

SOAKING AND COOKING PULSES

Pulses are easy to cook, but all except lentils and split peas need long soaking before being boiled and all except lentils and split peas need 10 minutes' fast boiling to destroy toxins. Don't add salt to the boiling water as this will toughen the pulses. Do use fresh water, not the soaking water, to boil pulses.

For all pulses, put them in a heavy saucepan with plenty of water to cover, boil fast uncovered for at least 10 minutes, then cover and simmer for the remainder of the cooking time.

The cooking times given opposite are only a guide, as the older the pulse the longer it will take to cook. After the time stated here, take a bean out and try it. Carry on cooking until it is soft, and use in the recipes in the following chapters or in your own recipes.

22

Cooked pulses will keep, covered, in the fridge for a few days or can be frozen, although they will often go mushy once thawed (which may be fine if you are using them for pâtés or dips, etc).

PULSE	SOAKING TIME	FAST BOILING TIME	SIMMERING TIME
Adzuki beans	8 hours	10 minutes	40 minutes
Black beans	8 hours	10 minutes	50 minutes
Black-eye beans	6 hours	10 minutes	40 minutes
Borlotti beans	8 hours	10 minutes	50 minutes
Broad beans	8 hours	10 minutes	1½ hours
Butter beans	8 hours	10 minutes	1 hour
Cannellini beans	8 hours	10 minutes	45 minutes
Flageolet beans	6 hours	10 minutes	45 minutes
Ful medames	8 hours	10 minutes	1 hour
Haricot beans	overnight	10 minutes	1½ hours
Kidney beans	overnight	10 minutes	50 minutes
Lima beans	8 hours	10 minutes	1 hour
Mung beans	8 hours	10 minutes	40 minutes
Pinto beans	8 hours	10 minutes	50 minutes
Soya beans	overnight	10 minutes	2–3 hours
Chickpeas	overnight	10 minutes	1½ hours
Split peas	NO	NO	30–45 minutes
Whole peas	8 hours	10 minutes	1½ hours
Lentils	NO	NO	30–45 minutes

Note: If you have a pressure cooker you can cook your pulses in it – no need for fast boiling, and reduce all simmering times by approximately two-thirds.

NUTS AND SEEDS

Although nuts and seeds are high-fat foods, apart from coconut they are low in saturated fat and have good protein and vitamin content, so it is worth keeping a few varieties of nut in the cupboard. Remember, however, that they don't last forever, even kept in their shells – they dry out and can be rancid, so try to eat them within a few weeks. Also watch out that the nuts you buy aren't salted!

The most useful nuts for cooking are *almonds* (whole and flaked), *walnut pieces and halves*, *cashews*, *peanuts* and *pistachios*. *Chestnuts* are worth a special mention as they, along with *hazelnuts*, are lower in fat than other varieties and make a good stuffing or loaf mixture.

Pine nuts are delicious in small quantities in many recipes – in salads, risotti and, of course, in Italian pesto sauce. *Sunflower* and *sesame seeds* are useful in all kinds of recipes, and sunflower seeds also make a good snack.

Many people like to toast or dry-fry their nuts and seeds before use as this intensifies their flavour.

Fresh *coconut* is best reserved for special occasions, as it is high in saturated fat. However, *desiccated coconut* goes a long way sprinkled on desserts or used in bakes or Indian dishes. You can also use fresh coconut to make coconut milk for Indonesian dishes – all you do is strain grated fresh coconut with water, pressing hard on the flesh until you have a milky liquid. This is quite time-consuming, however, and many people prefer to buy ready-made coconut milk.

TO SPROUT PULSES AND SEEDS

You can buy fresh beansprouts in the supermarket and sometimes these are fine, but other times they are not as young and fresh as they could be. If this is the case or you are fed up with only one variety (the Chinese mung bean type), why not sprout your own?

You can buy sprouting trays in layers, which you simply water each day until the sprouts appear. You can, however, sprout seeds almost as easily in a seed tray with drainage holes. Simply line the trays with nylon mesh, soak the seeds first (see list below for soaking times) and then sprinkle the seeds evenly on the mesh. Put in a warm dark place and spray with fresh water occasionally to keep the seeds moist until they sprout (usually in about three days, although some seeds can take up to six days).

Eat the sprouts when the shoots are 1–2 cm / ½–¾ in long, but let them stand in the light (eg on a windowsill) for a few hours before eating. The sprouts can be rinsed and stored in the fridge for several days in a plastic bag.

You can sprout all kinds of pulses and seeds; if sprouting two or three different types together, it is best to choose ones that take about the same time to germinate.

Alfalfa, black-eye beans, chickpeas and whole lentils take approximately 5 days, mung beans, mustard seeds and wheat take about 4 days and millet, oats, sesame seeds, soya beans and sunflower seeds, about 3 days.

SOAKING TIMES
6 hours – alfalfa and sesame
8 hours – lentils, soya beans
Overnight (at least 12 hours) – black-eye beans, chickpeas, millet, mung beans, oats, sunflower seeds, wheat.
Radish and mustard seeds don't need any soaking.

DAIRY PRODUCTS AND SUBSTITUTES

If you use dairy produce, remember that many cheeses, cream, ice-cream and, to a lesser extent, whole milk and whole-milk yogurts are high-fat foods. The rule, therefore, should be – buy lower-fat alternatives as often as you can and use the high-fat versions sparingly. If you want to cut dairy produce down – or even out – there are very reasonable alternatives for everything.

MILK

As it contains virtually no fat, skimmed milk is the sensible choice for everyday use (except for infants, who should drink whole milk until they are five).

Soya milk is the alternative for vegans – it has comparable nutrients, and no more calories than skimmed milk. Soya milk is often fortified with extra calcium or vitamin B12. Read the label carefully to make sure there is no added sugar.

YOGURT

Natural low-fat yogurt is best for everyday use as it is low in fat and calories. You can buy it either set or runny, or you can buy low-fat Bio yogurt which is supposed to contain the live cultures said to keep your digestive system running smoothly. It has a very mild taste and would be first choice if you normally don't much care for natural yogurt.

Otherwise make your own using the recipe on page 122. Buy whole milk or Greek-style strained yogurt for special occasions, to use in recipes (the extra fat in them helps prevent the yogurt from curdling when heated) or as a dessert topping or soup garnish instead of cream.

If you buy fruit yogurt and low-calorie fruit yogurts and you are a committed vegetarian, you should read the ingredients labels carefully as some contain products of animal origin, such as gelatine (for non-vegetarian E numbers, see list on page 29). Vegans will find low-fat soya 'yogurt' or fruit soya yogurt in the health-food shops as alternatives.

CREAM

Try to avoid double cream, whipping cream, clotted cream and soured cream, except as rare treats – they are *really high-fat* foods and there are lighter and just as enjoyable alternatives, such as *extra thick single cream*, *crème fraîche*, *natural fromage frais* and *Greek-style yogurt*.

Vegans will find soya 'cream' in the health-food shops, which can be used in any recipe that calls for cream.

CHEESE

Many hard cheeses are made with animal rennet, which isn't suitable for committed vegetarians. However, more and more non-animal-rennet cheeses are now widely available. As I write, you can get *non-animal-rennet Cheddar*, *low-fat Cheddar*, *Stilton*, *Cheshire* and *Parmesan*. Most of the soft cheeses don't use animal rennet anyway. All *cottage cheeses*, *low-fat soft cheeses*, *Mozzarella*, *goats' cheeses*, *Feta*, *Haloumi* and *Ricotta* should be rennet-free.

As a rule of thumb, when buying a hard cheese from a supermarket, if it doesn't say 'suitable for vegetarians' on the label it probably does contain animal rennet. Your local health-food store may stock a wider variety of rennet-free cheeses, so it is worth checking that out – the assistant is likely to be helpful in telling you which cheeses from the un-prepacked cheese counter are animal-rennet-free.

In practice, many vegetarians do eat animal-rennet cheeses, but this is changing as more become available.

For your waistline's and health's sake, it is wise to limit the full-fat cheeses – such as Cheddar, Stilton and cream cheese – to celebratory or occasional use and to get in the habit of buying more of the lower-fat kinds. As I write, there is at least one brand of reduced-fat vegetarian Cheddar available and the medium- and low-fat cheeses such as Ricotta and Quark are good in cooking. Buy a lump of Parmesan and keep it wrapped in the fridge for use in cooking – when grated, a little goes a very long way indeed, so you needn't feel guilty about that.

EGGS

Eggs are a nutritious food, but quite high in fat; so limit yourself to a few a week. Most vegetarians prefer to buy free-range eggs – both from the moral point of view and because they do taste better.

ICE-CREAM

Various reduced-fat ice-creams are now available, most of which taste quite good and, if you are an ice-cream addict, provide a much lower-calorie, lower-fat treat than the full-fat kinds. For vegans, you can buy soya ice-cream.

FATS AND MARGARINES

Butter is suitable for vegetarians, but you will have to become an avid label-reader if you want to eat margarine, low-fat spread or any of the new crop of spreads because not all of them are totally vegetarian – some contain fish oils, others contain non-vegetarian E numbers.

Vegans will have to be ever more careful as many vegetable-based spreads and margarines do contain some dairy products, eg whey. Your health-food store is likely to be a good source of true vegetarian and vegan spreads and margarines.

If you are vegan and can't find a suitable low-fat spread, you can make your own by blending true vegan margarine with an equal quantity of water in an electric blender, putting it into containers and storing, covered, in the fridge.

VEGETABLE PROTEINS

If you don't eat dairy produce, or if you want to keep your dairy intake as low at possible, it is a good idea to buy one or two vegetable protein products.

Tofu is a high-protein food made from soya beans. You buy it in blocks, usually shrink-wrapped, from the chilled counters. It comes in various types: firm and soft (both fine for slicing and using in stir-fries, etc), silken (best for using in dips and sauces although I like its delicate flavour in stir-fries), and smoked (good for kebabs). Tofu tastes quite bland but different brands vary in taste and texture, so try them until you find one that appeals to you.

Myco-protein is a newer protein food made from a type of edible fungus. Low in fat, you can buy it from the chilled cabinets in chunks or as mince. Its brand name is 'Quorn', and it can be used in stews, casseroles, bakes, pies, stir-fries, etc.

Dried *TVP* (Textured Vegetable Protein) is available in various brands at the supermarket as dried mince or chunks and unbranded at the health-food shop. Sometimes you can get dark and light varieties. TVP is supposed to taste similar to meat, which will only be of use to people who like the taste of meat and want to be reminded of it. You reconstitute it with water and use it in place of meat in recipes.

There are various other high-protein products available. Most you will probably only find at your health-food shop. There is *miso* – a dark moist crumbly product made from fermented soya beans. Its best use is to add flavour and colour to stocks, stews and soups, though it can be rather salty. *Yeast extract* is made from brewers' yeast and salt and should be used sparingly as a flavouring.

FRUIT AND VEGETABLES

As a healthy vegetarian diet should contain plenty of fresh fruit and vegetables, you will want to experiment with new varieties, not just rely on old favourites.

The bigger supermarkets are, in my experience, the best place to find unusual and exotic varieties all year round. They normally also have the freshest stock and almost all now have an organic section.

Never buy fruit or vegetables that look discoloured, limp, wilted, bruised, dried out, or that have been displayed under a hot sun. Fresh fruit and veg will be your major source of vitamin C, which is destroyed by light, heat and long storage. Sadly, I still find that too many health-food stores carry fresh produce well past its best.

Most fruit (except bananas) and most vegetables will keep much better, for longer, and retain their vitamins, if kept in the fridge once home. If you don't have fridge space for all your fresh produce, do at least keep it in the coolest, darkest conditions you can. Leaves will keep for longer if stored in plastic bags.

If you buy fresh – with fruit, even slightly under-ripe – and store well, most varieties of fruit and vegetables should keep for more or less a week (carrots and potatoes will keep for longer). So there is no need to do more than a weekly shop – especially if you plan out your week's menus in advance and shop carefully.

Also don't forget to buy in season and freeze surplus for the winter months when you may find less choice.

DRIED FRUIT AND VEGETABLES

Keep a selection of dried fruit in airtight tins in your larder. All dried fruit is a good source of fibre and most is a good source of iron, though none has any vitamin C left. Buy some 'no-need-to-soak' dried fruits which can be chopped into breakfast yogurt or cereals, and buy some packs that you can soak for a few hours and then simmer for a short while to give a delicious compote that can be used as a breakfast, dessert or snack. *Prunes*, *dried apricots* and *peaches* are the best source of nutrients, but *dried apples*, *pears*, *figs* and *currants* add variety.

It is worth keeping a small selection of *dried mushrooms* in your larder. Reconstituted Chinese mushrooms are essential for Far-Eastern cooking, while wild mushrooms of all kinds add interest and flavour to risotti, salads, and soups. I don't see much point in keeping dried onion as fresh onions, well stored, last a long time.

HERBS

I consider a selection of fresh and dried herbs essential for any cook and the vegetarian is no exception. At the minimum you should try to have a regular supply of fresh *parsley*, *mint*, *basil*, *chives*, *coriander*, *rosemary*, *sage*, *thyme* and *garlic*. You can either sow the seed yourself or buy small pots from the supermarket or garden centre to put on your window-shelf; or you can buy cut fresh leaves in packs, or perhaps in bunches from your greengrocer. Cut varieties need to be used within a day or two.

For times when you just can't get hold of a fresh herb, you can chop and freeze most varieties which, when thawed, will offer more flavour and aroma than dried herbs. Even so, there will still be times when you do have to fall back on dried varieties.

Keep dried herbs in opaque jars in a cool place and throw them out if they have been around more than a few months; as they will not do your cooking any favours.

SPICES

If you have a good health-food shop, it is probably best to buy your spices from there as prices will be much lower than at the supermarkets, who never seem to sell spices in large enough packs anyway!

Most spices are best bought whole and ground yourself as you need them. This is quite easily done using a pestle and mortar, or a blender with a grinding facility. The flavour and aroma of freshly ground spices is far superior to ready ground, long-stored varieties.

The spices worth stocking up with are *coriander seeds*, *cumin*, *dried whole ginger*, *dried whole chillies*, *saffron*, *turmeric*, *cloves* and *cardamom*. Buy *fresh ginger* and *fresh chillies* when you can.

Of course you will also want *black peppercorns* and it is useful to have a few spice 'mixtures' too, such as *Chinese five-spice powder* or *Thai seven-spice*.

CONDIMENTS AND OTHER INGREDIENTS

To make your cooking creative and delicious, here is a list of what I consider essential in the way of bottles, jars and cans you should keep in stock. You may well add some of your own, but all committed vegetarians should check labels carefully as not all condiments that seem to be vegetarian actually are. For instance, Worcestershire sauce contains anchovies, and Thai curry paste contains prawns.

Garlic purée: in tubes or jars is a handy standby and sometimes even better in a recipe than chopped fresh garlic.

Tomato purée: important for so many recipes.

Chopped tomatoes: when fresh tomatoes are all insipid or under-ripe, canned tomatoes are always a preferable alternative.

Passata: keep a couple of jars or packets of sieved tomato for sauces, bakes, casseroles; it is quite indispensable.

Worcestershire sauce: you can buy anchovy-free sauce at the health-food shop.

Black bean sauce and *yellow bean sauce*: these Far-Eastern soya bean condiments are ideal for quick stir-fries and for marinating tofu.

Plum sauce: another nice stir-fry addition.

Soy sauce: you can buy light or dark; shoyu is the natural and best soya.

Canned coconut milk: brands vary in their taste and their 'freshness' feel; try a few until you find one that tastes as good as freshly made coconut milk!

Yeast extract: adds taste and colour to stocks, soups, sauces, casseroles.

Sea salt: use freshly ground crystals sparingly in recipes.

Agar-agar: vegetarian alternative to gelatine, available from health food stores.

Stock cubes: most vegetable stock cubes aren't terrific – they seem very salty for one thing – but it may be useful to have a small pack for emergencies. Otherwise you can use yeast extract or 'Vecon' in a jar. You can also buy cartons of chilled vegetable stock which may be better than using stock cubes. These stocks will also freeze.

Canned peppers: I keep one can of mixed peppers for use with tomato or courgettes in ratatouilles or stir-fries as a quick side vegetable. I also keep a can of piquillo peppers – delicious Spanish peppers that are costly but make a superb starter, just drizzled with a little olive oil and dusted with black pepper.

Canned artichoke hearts: keep a jar or can for starters, mixed salads and rice salads, for roasting with other vegetables – in fact they have dozens of delicious uses!

Pickles and chutneys: a jar of good-quality chutney livens up a quick lunch of crusty bread and cheese; a good aubergine or lime relish goes well with all Eastern dishes. Your health-food store will have a wide selection.

Water chestnuts: have a can ready to give crunch to vegetable stir-fries.

Bamboo shoots: also good in Chinese stir-fries.

Oils: you will, of course, want some good-quality olive oil for salads and perhaps some mid-quality for cooking. You will also need sunflower oil for a lighter taste in certain recipes. Oriental sesame oil (made from roasted seeds) is the best oil to use for Eastern dishes, while walnut oil makes a nice salad dressing. Keep a bottle of corn oil for general-purpose cooking.

Store oils in cool dark conditions and use fairly quickly – walnut oil, in particular, goes rancid within weeks.

Vinegars: have a stock of three or four vinegars. You don't need malt vinegar, but have a good red wine and white wine vinegar, plus a cider vinegar and a sherry vinegar. They last for ages and are good for dressings, marinades and all kinds of dishes.

SWEETENERS

A little sugar isn't going to do you any harm, so keep some by. Brown sugar isn't particularly any better than white, so the choice is yours. Fructose (fruit sugar) is indispensable for cooking, as it is twice as sweet as sucrose (sugar) and isn't absorbed into the bloodstream so quickly. Unless you are a strict vegan you will also want some runny honey.

SHORT CUTS TO GOOD FOOD

For the cook in a hurry, there are various ways you can save time in the vegetarian kitchen:

★ Use ready-cooked canned pulses, rather than soaking and boiling your own.

★ Invest in a pressure cooker to cut down time on cooking soups, stews, beans and vegetables.

★ You can buy ready-cooked and frozen rice as a standby. It isn't quite as good as your own rice, but can be pepped up with a few additions.

★ Think 'pasta': keep a good stock of pasta shapes and varieties; all cook within about 12 minutes and provide delicious, nutritious suppers with …

★ Sauces! When you aren't so busy, batch-cook some sauces (eg tomato, lentil, spinach) and freeze them. You can even stock a couple of ready-made sauces in jars – some Italian pasta sauces are quite good and carton ones from the chilled counter at the supermarket are even better. Not all are low in fat, so check the label.

★ Microwave – I have never managed to achieve brilliant results cooking recipes from scratch in a microwave cooker. They are, however, very useful for defrosting sauces, soups, fruit purées and breads that it is worth investing in a small basic one if you are permanently busy or have a lone vegetarian in the household. With a microwave, baked potatoes can be cooked in a few minutes and topped with a sauce or fromage frais.

★ For cold weather: soups and stir-fries. Many of the soup recipes in this book are quick to do, as are many of the suppers and lunches. When cooking a recipe that will freeze, always make double the quantity to provide you with an instant ready meal for another day.

★ For hot weather: bread and cheese or bread and a spread or dip such as those on pages 63–6 are quick and ideal. Add salad for a perfect balanced meal.

★ Eggs: if you eat eggs, a frittata-style (flat) omelette with vegetables is quick and delicious once or twice a week, as is a soufflé omelette or scrambled eggs with herbs or coriander and bread.

NON-VEGETARIAN INGREDIENTS AND E NUMBERS

Non-vegetarian ingredients: cochineal, pepsin, gelatine, glycerine, hydrolysed proteins, rennet, glycerol, aspic, stearates.

Notes: hydrolysed vegetable protein is all right. Sometimes lecithin (often added to margarine and chocolate) is produced from battery eggs, so is not always suitable for vegans or lacto-vegetarians.

E numbers: the following commonly used food additives may be obtained from either plant or animal sources – it is almost impossible to be sure, therefore, that foods containing these E numbers are totally vegetarian unless the manufacturer can provide you with information: E120 (cochineal), 153, 203, 213, 226, 263, 302, 304, 327, 333, 334, 338–41, 352, 385, 404, 422, 431, 435, 450, 470, 471, 482, 492, 509, 516, 526, 529, 540, 545, 552, 570, 572, 623, 627, 631.

Planning your own diet

Here you will find out how to balance your own daily diet – for good health as well as enjoyment – and put into practice all the ideas you learned in the previous chapters.

At the start of this book we looked at the different elements that go to make up a healthy well-balanced vegetarian diet. How do you translate all that knowledge into enjoyable daily and weekly menus?

I have devised the five plans that appear later in this chapter as examples of some of the many different and delicious ways you can eat to suit yourself, secure in the knowledge that you are eating within World Heath Organization guidelines.

The seven-day plans show how the recipes from the later chapters of the book can be incorporated into a healthy overall diet which will be high in carbohydrates and fibre, low in fat, and with adequate protein, vitamins and minerals. If you need to lose weight, turn to the next chapter.

By using one or two of these plans and trying out the different recipes you will soon get a 'feel' for eating a vegetarian diet that is not only pleasurable but also nutritious and well balanced. The plans are all suitable in calorie content for most women to maintain their current weight. Men may need to add extra calories in the form of more bread, potatoes, rice, cereals and pulses to one or two meals a day, or take extra between-meal snacks of these foods and perhaps some extra fruit.

When you've tried out some of the plans that best suit you, you will of course want to begin building your own daily and weekly menus. You can be sure of getting a healthy diet if you stick to the following common-sense principles:
* Build each meal – or at least most of them – around a high-carbohydrate food (such as rice or another grain, pasta, potatoes, beans, bread and pizza).
* Add some high-protein, low-fat food to this basic food if necessary. Remember that most of the high-carbohydrate foods

(such as pulses and whole grains) are also good sources of protein in themselves. If adding dairy produce, add only small amounts.

These first two ingredients of the meal will together almost certainly form your 'complete' protein (see pages 10–11).

High-protein foods you may like to add include tofu, egg, cheese, skimmed milk and soya milk. Higher in fat are nuts and seeds, which should be added in moderation.

* Now add plenty of lightly cooked fresh vegetables or raw salads.

* Add fruit to most meals. If the 'main course' has been fairly low in protein, you can add a low-fat, high-protein dessert, such as fromage frais or yogurt.

If you keep choosing first a large portion of carbohydrate, and then add a smaller amount of protein foods and plenty of fruit and vegetables, you can't go wrong!
EXAMPLES:
BREAKFAST
1   Choose a high-carbohydrate food, such as a whole grain cereal.
2   Add high-protein skimmed milk or soya milk.
3   Add a piece of fresh fruit.
LUNCH
1   Choose a high-carbohydrate food, like a baguette.
2   Add a high-protein food, eg lentil pâté.
3   Add a large mixed salad.
(You could also add some yogurt or a piece of fresh fruit to this meal.)
EVENING
1   Choose a high-carbohydrate food, like rice.
2 and 3   Add a high-protein food and fresh vegetables, eg tofu and vegetable stir-fry.
(You could add fresh fruit to this meal.)
OR
Choose one of the ready-balanced recipe dishes that appear in the chapters on Quick Suppers and Lunches (page 70) or Main Courses (page 82). This may be a complete meal in itself or there may be serving suggestions with it – or you could pick one of the meal suggestions from one of the plans (pages 35–9 and 45–9).

If you don't have to worry about your weight at all (some people can eat lots more than others without ever gaining weight), then you can also add one of the healthy desserts from the Sweet Treats chapter (see page 106), or

something else of your own. You could instead perhaps even snack on some of the healthy bakes in that same chapter between meals.

The only other 'rules' to bear in mind are that all fats and oils should be added sparingly to foods. For example, don't coat your hunk of bread with a slab of butter as a matter of habit, or you will be undoing the good that the rest of your healthy diet is doing you! Use fat only when really necessary to add flavour, brown and seal food or add moisture, as in a dressing.

It is also important not to stick to the same few food items day in and day out – experiment with new foods, new recipes, new fruits and vegetables and you are bound to get all the nutrients you need for health.

USING THE RECIPES

Many of the main meal, supper and lunch recipes in the later chapters are perfectly balanced nutritionally – high in carbohydrate, low in fat and with adequate protein, vitamins and minerals. However, the proportions of these constituents do vary, and so each recipe incorporates a nutrition information panel to help you build your balanced diet. Here is an explanation of how to use these in working out a healthy daily diet:

* CALORIE counts are self-explanatory. If female, build a diet based on around 2,000 calories a day; if male, on around 2,700 a day.

* TOTAL FAT content is given as 'High', 'Medium' or 'Low'. 'High' means that the recipe contains over 35% total fat content (of total calorie content of the recipe). In most cases, any recipe included in this book with a high total fat content will be eaten with a low-fat, high-carbohydrate accompaniment (eg bread with a high-fat dip.) However, by most standards, none of the recipes in this book is very high in fat – otherwise it wouldn't have been included. 'Medium' fat content means the recipe contains between 20 and 35% fat. If the carbohydrate content of a medium-fat meal is high, it will then give you a reasonably well balanced meal in itself. 'Low' means the recipe contains less than 20% fat and if you choose such a dish you could then, perhaps, add another higher-fat dish to the menu without feeling guilty (eg a bake or dessert, or some grated cheese).

* SATURATED FAT content is also given. This is because it is the saturated fats in our diet we should be

making most efforts to cut down – the WHO has given a level of saturated fat of 10% of the total daily calories as ideal. Here, therefore, 'high' means the recipe contains over 10% of its total calories as saturated fat; 'medium' means it contains from 5 to 10%, and 'low' means it contains less than 5%. These saturated fat figures are, of course, not in addition to the total fat figures.

★ CARBOHYDRATE content is given as 'High', 'Medium' or 'Low'. 'High' means that the recipe contains over 50% of its calories as carbohydrate, 'medium' means between 40 and 50%, and 'low' means it contains less than 40%. You will find that the 'low-carbohydrate' recipes are virtually always to be eaten with high-carbohydrate accompaniments (eg bread, rice or potatoes).

Any high-carbohydrate savoury dish will also be high in fibre. Some of the bakes and desserts are not necessarily high in fibre as their carbohydrate content may be in the form of simple sugars or fructose that contain no fibre. However, these recipes are intended to be eaten in small quantities and so there is no need to worry about including them in your diet.

★ PROTEIN content is given as 'High', 'Medium' or 'Low'. 'High' means the recipe contains over 15% of its calories as protein, 'medium' means it contains between 5 and 15%, 'low' means it contains under 5%. As normal protein intake averages out at around 10–15% a day, you could balance a low-protein meal with a high-protein meal at another time of day, or add on a high-protein dessert or drink.

★ CHOLESTEROL content is given in milligrams for people who have been advised by their doctor to keep a check on their blood cholesterol levels. For most of us it is more important to watch our fat intake levels and get enough fruit and vegetables.

★ VITAMINS are named when that particular vitamin is found in good quantities in that recipe. The vitamins are listed starting with the one found in most quantity and so on. Vitamins other than those listed may be present in the recipe, but not in such significant amounts.

★ MINERALS are listed in the same manner as vitamins.

As I said earlier, if you are getting a wide variety of foods you should automatically get all the vitamins and minerals you need for good health, but if you would like to make sure, these nutritional information panels give you a more thorough check.

Now, if you need to lose some weight or have someone in the family who would like to slim, turn to the next chapter!

THE VEGAN PLAN

*Seven days of tempting meals with no dairy produce at all.
About 2,000 calories per day*

Extras per day: 250 ml / 8 fl oz soya milk, 2 glasses of wine or 200 calories' worth of any cake or bake from the Sweet Treats chapter (page 106), 15 g / ½ oz vegetable margarine for use on bread and/or as a garnish.

Stuffed Vegetables

DAY ONE
BREAKFAST
2 *Reduced-fat Scones* with
  pure fruit spread
1 orange

LUNCH
Avocado and Leaf Salad
1 large wholemeal roll
1 large banana

EVENING
Delhi-style Cauliflower
  (made using soya 'yogurt')
Chana Masaledar
140 g / 5 oz boiled brown
  rice
chutney of choice
fresh sliced mango, dressed
  with lime juice and served
  with non-dairy cream

DAY TWO
BREAKFAST
American-style Granola with
  soya milk (extra to
  allowance)
1 apple or peach

LUNCH
Avocado and Tofu Dip with
  crudités
Black Bean Soup with 75 g /
  3 oz French bread
ready-made soya 'yogurt'
  dessert

EVENING
Guacamole with toasted
  bread sticks
Vegetable Paella
Marinated Strawberries

DAY THREE
BREAKFAST
200 g / 7 oz baked beans on
  2 large slices of
  wholemeal toast
1 orange

LUNCH
75 g / 3 oz egg-free pasta of
  choice (dry weight), boiled
  and topped with
Tomato Sauce
50 g / 2 oz nuts and raisins

EVENING
Spicy Stuffed Vegetables
*Baked Banana with Lemon
  and Orange*
1 portion of soya 'ice-cream'

DAY FOUR
BREAKFAST
Fruit Compote
1 slice of *Banana and
  Walnut Teabread*
1 glass of orange juice

LUNCH
1 slice of cold *Cashew Roast*
large mixed salad
110 g / 4 oz cooked new
  potatoes or brown rice
*Orange and Watercress
  Salad*

EVENING
Cobbler-topped Casserole
1 large portion of leafy
  greens, lightly cooked
one 175 g / 6 oz baked
  potato
1 cooking apple, cored and
  filled with dried fruit of
  choice and 1 dessertspoon
  brown sugar, then baked

DAY FIVE
BREAKFAST
1 glass of orange juice
2 *Reduced-fat Scones* with
  Banana Spread

LUNCH
*Brown Rice Salad with
  Mushrooms and Beans*
1 wholemeal roll
1 kiwi fruit or peach

EVENING
Three-bean Casserole
one 140 g / 5 oz sweet
  potato, baked
large mixed salad with *Oil-
  free Vinegar Dressing*
Baked Peaches with soya
  'ice-cream'

DAY SIX
BREAKFAST
Special Recipe Muesli with
  soya milk (extra to
  allowance)
½ portion of *Fruit Compote*

LUNCH
1 glass of orange juice
Lentil Pâté with 75 g / 3 oz
  crusty bread
Fruit Coleslaw
1 large banana

EVENING
Italian Artichokes
1 wholemeal roll
75 g / 3 oz egg-free pasta
  (dry weight), boiled, with
Mediterranean Sauce and
  1 tablespoon pine nuts
  sprinkled over

DAY SEVEN
BREAKFAST
2 slices of bread with
  Cashew Nut Spread
1 orange
½ portion of *Fruit Compote*

LUNCH
*Curried Lentil and Vegetable
  Soup*
2 *Scottish Oatcakes*
100 g / 3½ oz grapes or
  plums

EVENING
Marinated Mushrooms
1 slice of rye or wholemeal
  bread
Bombay Supper
2 poppadums
1 apple

Plums

FAST AND SIMPLE

In this seven-day plan the accent is on meals that are easy and quick to prepare and cook. You can save more time by buying in muesli, oatcakes and teabread, but all three recipes are quick and easy.
About 2,000 calories per day

Extras per day: 250 ml / 8 fl oz skimmed milk, 2 glasses of wine or 200 calories' worth of any cake or bake from the Sweet Treats chapter (page 106) or similar, 15 g / ½ oz butter or vegetable margarine for use on bread and/or as a garnish.

Pasta spirals with spinach sauce

DAY ONE
BREAKFAST
2 *Scottish Oatcakes* with *Banana Spread*
1 pear or peach
1 portion of natural low-fat yogurt with 1 teaspoon runny honey

LUNCH
2 slices of wholemeal bread filled with 1 tablespoon peanut butter and salad
1 orange

EVENING
Summer Frittata
large mixed salad
75 g / 3 oz French bread
Fruit Coleslaw

DAY TWO
BREAKFAST
2 slices of bread, toasted and topped with *Cashew Nut Spread*
1 glass of grapefruit or mixed citrus fruit juice
1 portion of natural low-fat yogurt with 1 teaspoon of runny honey

LUNCH
Lentil Pâté with 1 large wholemeal roll
Chicory, Orange and Date Salad
1 large banana

EVENING
75 g / 3 oz pasta spirals (dry weight), boiled, with *Spinach Sauce* and 2 tablespoons grated Parmesan cheese
1 apple

DAY THREE
BREAKFAST
American-style Granola with milk (extra to allowance)
1 glass of orange juice
1 slice of wholemeal bread with pure fruit spread

LUNCH
Mushroom Spread on 3 slices of rye crispbread
Leek and Chive Soup
1 peach or pear
1 slice of *Caribbean Teacake*

EVENING
Hot Cheese and Olive Platter
1 large crusty roll
1 large banana

DAY FOUR
BREAKFAST
1 large portion of low-fat natural yogurt sprinkled with ½ portion of *Special Recipe Muesli* and 1 piece of fresh fruit of choice, chopped or 110 g / 4 oz soft fruit

LUNCH
Baguette spread with *Mexican-style Dip* and filled with crisp lettuce and tomato

EVENING
Tofu Kebabs with Peanut Sauce
60 g / 2½ oz (dry weight) Thai fragrant rice, boiled
Hazelnut Ice-cream

DAY FIVE
BREAKFAST
2 Weetabix with skimmed milk (extra to allowance)
1 large slice of bread with pure fruit spread
1 apple

LUNCH
1 large crusty roll filled with *Red Lentil Spread*
Fruit Coleslaw
1 fruit yogurt

EVENING
Chinese Egg and Noodle Stir-fry
1 portion of lychees with 1 small tub of fromage frais

DAY SIX
BREAKFAST
Special Recipe Muesli with skimmed milk (extra to allowance)
1 glass of orange juice

LUNCH
100 g / 3½ oz cooked brown rice mixed with ½ ripe chopped avocado and 1 portion of *Fresh Tomato Salsa*
75 g / 3 oz crusty bread

EVENING
Three-bean Casserole
one 200 g / 7 oz baked potato
lightly cooked broccoli or mange-tout peas
Baked Banana with Lemon and Orange

DAY SEVEN
BREAKFAST
As Day Three

LUNCH
3 oatcakes with 50 g / 2½ oz Brie or Camembert or half-fat vegetarian Cheddar cheese
large tomato and onion salad
1 slice of *Caribbean Teacake*

EVENING
Tagliatelle with Wine and Mushrooms
large mixed leaf salad with *Oil-free Vinegar Dressing*
selection of fruits with 1 tablespoon Greek-style yogurt or crème fraîche

THE FAMILY PLAN

Robust and interesting meals that all the family will enjoy.
About 2,000 calories per day

Extras per day: 250 ml / 8 fl oz skimmed milk (full-fat milk for children under 5), 2 glasses wine or 200 calories' worth of any cake or bake from the Sweet Treats chapter (page 106), 15 g / ½ oz butter or vegetable margarine for use on bread and/or as a garnish.

Baked apples with sultanas + honey

DAY ONE
BREAKFAST
American-style Granola with
  skimmed milk (extra to
  allowance) with
1 large banana chopped in
1 glass of orange juice
1 apple

LUNCH
*Curried Lentil and Vegetable
  Soup* (for small children
  you can omit most of the
  curry powder)
1 pitta bread
1 fruit-flavoured fromage
  frais

EVENING
*Macaroni, Red Pepper and
  Broccoli Bake*
1 portion of green leafy
  vegetable, lightly cooked
2 *Peach and Raisin Cookies*

DAY TWO
BREAKFAST
1 glass of orange juice
Fruit Compote
1 portion of natural low-fat
  yogurt

LUNCH
Pistou with 75 g / 3 oz rye
  bread
1 peach or pear

EVENING
*Cheese and Onion Bread
  Bake* or *Hereford Hot-pot*
green salad
1 baked apple, cored and
  filled with sultanas and
  honey
1 portion of natural
  fromage frais

DAY THREE
BREAKFAST
2 large tomatoes, sliced and
  grilled on 1 large slice of
  wholemeal toast
1 glass of apple juice
1 large banana

LUNCH
Guacamole with crudités
*Classic Three-bean Salad
  with Pasta*

EVENING
Aubergine and Lentil Layer
50 g / 2 oz (dry weight)
  brown rice, boiled
mixed salad
stewed fruit, such as apricots
  with 2 tablespoons Greek-
  style yogurt

DAY FOUR
BREAKFAST
Special Recipe Muesli with
  skimmed milk (extra to
  allowance) and
2 pieces of fresh fruit of
  choice, chopped in

LUNCH
Parsley and Potato Soup
Red Lentil Spread on 2 slices
  of wholemeal toast
salad of fresh beansprouts
  mixed with grated
  beetroot and apple, all
  tossed in *Light Vinaigrette*

EVENING
*Provençal Pancakes with
  Cheese Sauce*
green leaf salad
fresh fruit salad with
  2 tablespoons of Greek-
  style yogurt

DAY FIVE
BREAKFAST
2 *Pineapple Muffins*
1 orange

LUNCH
275 g / 10 oz baked potato
  with *Chana Masaledar*
large mixed salad

EVENING
Crispy Vegetable Pie
175 g / 6 oz new potatoes
1 portion of leafy greens
Summer Pudding
Greek-style yogurt

DAY SIX
BREAKFAST
2 slices of wholemeal bread
  with *Banana Spread*
1 portion of natural low-fat
  yogurt with 1 teaspoon
  runny honey
1 glass of orange juice

LUNCH
1 *Pizza Base* topped with
  Tomato Sauce, sliced
  mushrooms, deseeded
  and chopped green and
  yellow peppers and
  Mozzarella cheese
crisp green salad
1 slice of *Caribbean Teacake*

EVENING
Mexican-style Dip with toast
  fingers
Spicy Stuffed Vegetables
one 225 g / 8 oz baked
  potato
mixed salad
Fruit Compote with
  American-style Granola
  topping

DAY SEVEN
BREAKFAST
As Day Two

LUNCH
Leek and Chive Soup with
  ½ tablespoon sesame
  seeds or 25 g / 1 oz
  vegetarian Cheddar
  cheese grated on top
1 wholemeal roll
1 large banana

EVENING
75 g / 3 oz spaghettini (dry
  weight), boiled and
  topped with
Lentil Sauce
green salad
Hazelnut Ice-cream

LATE PREGNANCY

*In the first few months of pregnancy, you hardly need to eat any extra calories.
In the last few months, however, you should add around 300 calories a day
extra, and eat plenty of iron, calcium and vitamin C.*
About 2,300 calories per day

Extras per day: 500 ml / 16 fl oz skimmed milk, 100 g / 3½ oz natural low-fat yogurt
(with a little honey if you like), 200 calories' worth of cakes or bakes from the
Sweet Treats chapter (see page 106), 15 g / ½ oz butter or vegetable margarine for
use on bread and/or as a garnish.

Pea + watercress soup

DAY ONE
BREAKFAST
Special Recipe Muesli with
Fruit Compote and skimmed
milk (extra to allowance)
1 glass of orange juice

LUNCH
Marinated Mushrooms
Gado Gado
1 large banana
1 portion of fromage frais

EVENING
Falafel Patties
Fresh Tomato Salsa
1 wholemeal pitta bread
large mixed salad
Baked Peach

DAY TWO
BREAKFAST
1 large wholemeal roll
spread with yeast extract
1 small bowl of high-bran
cereal with skimmed milk
(extra to allowance)
1 orange

LUNCH
Cheese and Walnut Dip as a
spread in a large baguette
Winter Red Salad or tomato
and basil salad

EVENING
Polenta and Peppers
Tomato Sauce
mixed salad with *Light
Vinaigrette*
Marinated Strawberries with
Greek-style yogurt

DAY THREE
BREAKFAST
As Day One

LUNCH
Avocado and Tofu Dip with
crudités and strips of pitta
bread
Pea and Watercress Soup
1 *Pineapple Muffin*

EVENING
Broccoli and Sweetcorn Flan
200 g / 7 oz new potatoes or
cooked brown rice
green salad
salad of mixed fresh
beansprouts with sliced
raw mushrooms and *Oil-
free Vinegar Dressing*
*Baked Banana with Lemon
and Orange*

DAY FOUR
BREAKFAST
2 slices of wholemeal bread
1 large egg, boiled or
poached
1 orange
1 apple

LUNCH
Parsley and Potato Soup
1 baguette
1 large banana

EVENING
*Grilled Vegetables with
Bulghar*
Apricot Slice

DAY FIVE
BREAKFAST
As Day One

LUNCH
Summer Frittata
large slice of wholemeal
bread
large mixed salad
1 fruit-flavoured fromage
frais

EVENING
Mushroom Pilaff
green salad with *Light
Vinaigrette*
Lemon and Lime Sorbet

DAY SIX
BREAKFAST
As Day Two

LUNCH
large wholemeal baguette
filled with *Cashew Nut
Spread*
Fruit Coleslaw
1 banana

EVENING
*Provençal Pancakes with
Cheese Sauce*
green salad with *Light
Vinaigrette*
Fruit Compote with Greek-
style yogurt

DAY SEVEN
BREAKFAST
As Day Four

LUNCH
Spanish Chickpeas
1 pitta bread
green salad
Apricot Slice

EVENING
Rich Potato Bake
1 portion of lightly cooked
broccoli
Hazelnut Ice-cream

Grilled Vegetables

DINNER PARTY MENUS

Meat-eaters and non meat-eaters alike will enjoy these seven different vegetarian dinner party menus. Six of them have their own ethnic theme and one is specially devised for vegans.

With calorie counts as low as these – particularly the Spanish and Italian menus – you need not feel guilty about a glass or two of wine with the meal.

New potatoes + mint + chives

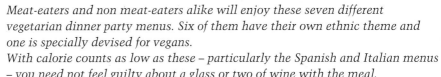

Mixed pepper Croustades

MENU THREE
BRITISH-STYLE

About 950 calories

Pea and Watercress Soup

* * * * *

Crispy Vegetable Pie
new potatoes with chopped
mint and chives
baby sweetcorn
mange-tout peas

* * * * *

Summer Pudding with extra-
thick single cream

MENU ONE
FAR-EASTERN STYLE

About 990 calories

Hot and Sour Soup

* * * * *

Thai-style Mixed Vegetables

Thai fragrant rice
Bakmie Goreng

* * * * *

Lemon and Lime Sorbet
fresh lychees

MENU TWO
INDIAN-STYLE

About 1,050 calories

Chana Masaledar with naan
bread

* * * * *

Bombay Supper
Delhi-style Cauliflower
yogurt with chopped
cucumber and fresh
chopped coriander
selection of chutneys

* * * * *

fresh mangoes and
kumquats

MENU FOUR
FRENCH-STYLE

About 1,000 calories

Marinated Aubergine and
Tomato

* * * * *

Cheese and Tomato Roulade
Hot Baby Vegetables with
Red Pesto
mixed leaf salad with *Oil-*
free Vinegar Dressing

* * * * *

meringue with *Marinated*
Strawberries and crème
fraîche

MENU FIVE
SPANISH-STYLE

About 900 calories

Mixed Pepper Croustades

* * * * *

Vegetable Paella
mixed leaf salad with *Light*
Vinaigrette

* * * * *

fresh fruit platter with a
selection of vegetarian
cheeses

MENU SIX
ITALIAN-STYLE

About 750 calories

Italian Artichokes

* * * * *

Tagliatelle with Wine and
Mushrooms
mixed salad

* * * * *

Baked Peaches with Italian
ice-cream

MENU SEVEN
VEGAN

About 720 calories

Avocado and Tofu Dip with
crudités

* * * * *

Carrot and Tomato Soup

* * * * *

Grilled Vegetables with
Bulghar
Orange and Watercress
Salad

* * * * *

Baked Bananas with Lemon
and Orange

Menu planning for weight loss

The vegetarian style of eating is very suitable for helping you to shed weight if you so wish. This chapter contains slimming plans and diet advice to make the process both pleasant and easy.

A recent UK Government Survey (*Health Survey for England, 1991*) shows that, despite the barrage of healthy eating advice that has been on offer for the past decade or more, the number of overweight and obese (very overweight) people in this country has risen since 1986.

On average, vegetarians are less likely than the rest of the population to suffer from obesity. So making the change from a carnivorous to a vegetarian diet should – if you tend to overweight – help you in your slimming campaign.

A few vegetarians, however, do put on weight – some, perhaps, because they don't take enough exercise; but others, I am sure, because they still eat a great deal of fat in the form of dairy produce, nuts and sweet pastries and cakes.

The slimming plans that follow show five different ways to combine the recipes in this book with other foods to allow you – or your partner or family – to slim successfully.

Look through the plans and if you happen to be a vegetarian with a weight problem you will see that there is no need to cut out all the foods you enjoy in order to lose weight. You can still have some dairy produce, cheese, desserts, bakes... the secret is to limit the overall fat and calorie content of your diet without going on a crash diet, so that you lose weight gradually.

A well-balanced vegetarian diet is ideally suited to help you lose weight without feeling deprived or wanting to give up for two main reasons:

1   It is (or should be) high in complex carbohydrates like bread, grains and pulses (see the first chapter for more information) – the very foods which, in all trials so far conducted, have been shown to help slimmers lose weight painlessly. This is because they actually appear to speed up your metabolic rate, helping you

to burn calories more quickly than if, say, you ate a low-calorie diet consisting mostly of fat. The complex carbohydrates also are high on filling power, so you don't feel hungry after eating your slimmer's meal. Thirdly, they keep you feeling full for longer so you don't get nagging between-meals hunger pangs and cravings.

2   It is (or should be) high in fresh fruits and vegetables, which will automatically add variety and colour and yet more filling power for a few extra calories. Their vitamins and minerals will also keep you healthy while you slim.

So, if you can just control your fat intake (with the help of my recipes in the chapters that follow) you have the perfect recipe for a successful diet!

Pick a plan that suits you and follow it for a week or two, and you will see how pleasant slimming can be. (See overleaf also for a list of foods that you can enjoy at any time on your diet in addition to all the foods in the plans.)

Then, perhaps, when you have lost a few pounds you will want to devise some diet plans of your own for more variety. In that case, these tips will help you:

★   First check out the height/weight chart on page 128 and see approximately how much weight you would like to lose (don't aim too low).

★   Remember that women should diet on around 1,200 calories a day; men and teenagers on around 1,500.

★   Split your daily calories over several meals or snacks, rather than having just, say, one big meal a day. This will stop you from feeling hungry.

★   All the recipes in this book are calorie-counted, so you can easily incorporate them into your own diet. The calorie counts of some of the more basic foods are given overleaf so that you can add them to the recipes or devise your own breakfasts, snacks, etc.

★   Make sure you have read the first chapter so that you understand the basics of getting a healthy diet – all the advice there applies just as much to you on a slimming diet. You keep the same balance – high carbohydrates, low fat and adequate protein – even though you are reducing the total calorie content of your diet.

★   Plan out at least several days' meals in advance.

★   Give yourself a daily skimmed or soya milk allowance and daily low-fat spread allowance – and stick to it.

★   It may help you plan your diet if you use a notebook to record what you intend to eat each day with its approximate calorie content.

BASIC FOODS CALORIE CHART

DAIRY PRODUCE
(per l00 ml / 3½ fl oz, unless otherwise stated)

skimmed milk	32
yogurt, natural low-fat	52
yogurt, strained Greek-style	132
yogurt, 1 tub diet fruit (125 ml / 4 fl oz)	50–60
fromage frais, natural 0% fat	48
fromage frais, 8% fat	112
fromage frais, diet fruit	45–50
crème fraîche (per 15 ml tablespoon)	55
single cream (per 15 ml tablespoon)	30
egg, 1 medium	80

CHEESES
(per 25 g / 1 oz, unless otherwise stated)

Cheddar, full fat	100
Cheddar, reduced-fat	62
cottage cheese	24
Brie	75
Danish blue	90
Edam	75
Feta	75
Mozzarella	62
Parmesan	110
Parmesan, grated (per 15 ml tablespoon)	30
Ricotta	40
low-fat soft cheese	33

SOYA PRODUCTS

soya milk (per l00 ml / 3½ fl oz)	32
soya yogurt (per 100 ml / 3½ fl oz)	50
soya cream (per 15 ml tablespoon)	30
tofu (per 25 g / 1 oz)	17
TVP (per 25 g / 1 oz reconstituted weight)	17

SWEETENERS AND SPREADS
(per 5 ml teaspoon)

sugar, all kinds	20
honey, all kinds	15
pure fruit spread	20

FATS

butter or margarine (per 25 g / 1 oz)	185
low-fat spread (per 25 g / 1 oz)	90
oils (per 15 ml tablespoon)	120

BREAKFAST CEREALS
(per 25 g / 1 oz, ie a small to medium bowlful, unless otherwise stated)

All Bran	68
Bran Flakes	80
Corn Flakes	90
Fruit 'n Fibre	90
Muesli*	82
Porridge (made with water)	44
Puffed Wheat	80
Shredded Wheat, one	80
Weetabix, one	65

* muesli is heavy, so an average bowlful is around 75 g / 3 oz

VEGETABLES
(per 25 g / 1 oz, unless otherwise stated)

leafy greens and most green vegetables	5
avocados (per half)	150
beetroot	10
carrots	6
parsnips	12
peas and fresh broad beans	13
potatoes, plain baked or boiled	20
red peppers	8
sweetcorn	30
sweet potatoes	20
tomatoes (1 average)	l0

GRAINS
(per 25 g / 1 oz dry weight uncooked)

flour, wholemeal	85
pasta	85
rice and other grains	90

PULSES
(per 25 g / 1 oz dry weight uncooked)

dried beans, most kinds	90
chickpeas	90
lentils	75
split peas	80

Note that dry grains and pulses absorb water during cooking so that 25 g / 1 oz dry weight will yield about 75 g / 3 oz cooked weight and that 75 g / 3 oz cooked weight will contain about the same calories as the 25 g / 1 oz dried.

NUTS AND SEEDS
(per 25 g / 1 oz shelled weight)

almonds, Brazils, peanuts, cashews, walnuts	about 150
chestnuts	42
hazelnuts	95
sunflower seeds	150
sesame seeds	150

DRIED FRUIT
(per 25 g / 1 oz)

peaches, apples, apricots, prunes	50
dates, sultanas, currants	65
figs	55

FRUITS

most single pieces of fruit, each	about 50
bananas, large, each	100
soft fruit (per 25 g / 1 oz), most kinds	7

UNLIMITED FOODS

All the following foods and items are unlimited on a slimming diet, whether you are devising your own diet or following one of the plans.
Vegetables (raw or lightly cooked without fat): beansprouts, bamboo shoots, cabbage (all kinds), cauliflower, celery, chicory, Chinese leaves or pak-choi, courgettes and marrow, cucumber, endive, fennel, lettuce (all kinds), mushrooms, mustard and cress, onions, green peppers, radicchio, radishes, watercress.
Herbs and spices: all fresh or dried herbs and spices.
Condiments, etc: capers, oil-free salad dressing, garlic purée, tomato purée, lemon juice, vinegar, gherkins.
To drink: water, mineral water, soda water, low-calorie soft drinks, herbal and fruit teas, tea and coffee (milk from allowance).

SLIMMING PLAN FOR VEGANS

The vegan diet is ideally suited to weight loss as it is naturally low in fat and high in fibre.
About 1,200 calories per day

Extras per day: 140 ml / ¼ pint soya milk for drinks, 15 g / ½ oz vegetarian low-fat spread.

Baked bananas with lemon + orange

DAY ONE
BREAKFAST
1 average bowlful of puffed wheat with 100 ml/ 3½ fl oz soya milk
1 banana

LUNCH
Carrot and Tomato Soup
1 wholemeal pitta with 50 g/2 oz hummus
chopped cucumber and spring onion

EVENING
Bombay Supper
1 orange mixed with 100 ml/3½ fl oz soya 'yogurt'

DAY TWO
BREAKFAST
½ portion *Special Recipe Muesli* with 100 ml/ 3½ fl oz soya milk and 1 kiwi fruit or peach chopped in

LUNCH
3 slices of rye crispbread
Mexican-style Dip (omitting cheese)
Fruit Coleslaw
25 g/1 oz nuts and raisins

EVENING
175 g/ 10 oz baked potato
Gumbo Creole
green salad
Baked Bananas with Lemon and Orange

DAY THREE
BREAKFAST
2 *Scottish Oatcakes*
1 glass of apple juice

LUNCH
Pasta Waldorf (made using tofu 'mayonnaise' and 25 g/1 oz extra walnuts instead of the cheese)
1 orange

EVENING
Three-bean Casserole
1 portion of purée of parsnips and potatoes
1 portion of broccoli
Baked Peach

DAY FOUR
BREAKFAST
½ portion of *Fruit Compote*
1 average slice of bread of choice with yeast extract or pure fruit spread

LUNCH
Leek and Chive Soup (made using soya milk and vegan margarine) or *Black Bean Soup*
65 g/2½ oz slice of French bread
1 apple

EVENING
Thai-style Mixed Vegetables with Chilli
50 g/2 oz (dry weight) grain of choice, boiled or steamed as appropriate
100 g/3½ oz grapes

DAY FIVE
BREAKFAST
American-style Granola with 100 ml/3½ fl oz soya milk (extra to allowance)
1 glass of orange juice

LUNCH
Mushroom Spread (made using 2 tablespoons soya milk instead of the fromage frais) on 1 wholemeal bap
large mixed salad with *Oil-free Vinegar Dressing*
40 g/1½ oz dried apricots

EVENING
Tofu Kebabs with Peanut Sauce
salad greens
1 wholemeal pitta bread
Marinated Strawberries

DAY SIX
BREAKFAST
1 large slice of wholemeal bread with *Apricot Spread*
1 apple

LUNCH
Guacamole with crudités and toast fingers or taco chips
1 slice of *Apple and Sultana Loaf*

EVENING
Mushroom Pilaff
green salad
mixed fresh citrus fruit

DAY SEVEN
BREAKFAST
banana whizz: mix in blender 1 chopped medium banana, 100 ml/ 3½ fl oz soya milk and 3 tablespoons orange juice
1 average slice of wholemeal bread with yeast extract

LUNCH
Cantonese Noodle Salad (made using egg-free noodles)
1 peach or nectarine

EVENING
Falafel Patties (made replacing the egg with a little soya milk to bind)
1 wholemeal pitta bread
Chicory, Orange and Date Salad
3 tablespoons soya 'ice-cream'

SPEEDY SLIMMING PLAN

This plan is ideal for busy singles or couples who want to lose weight. About 1,200 calories per day. All of the recipes in these plans are quick and easy to do.

Extras per day: 140 ml / ¼ pint skimmed milk for drinks, 15 g / ½ oz vegetarian low-fat spread.

Guacamole + crudités

Pizza avocado tomato sauce

DAY ONE
BREAKFAST
100 ml / 3½ fl oz low-fat natural yogurt with
   1 teaspoon runny honey
1 banana
100 ml / 3½ fl oz orange juice

LUNCH
200 g / 7 oz baked beans on
   2 slices of wholemeal toast or *Brown Rice Salad with Mushrooms and Beans*
green salad

EVENING
Bakmie Goreng
1 peach or nectarine
2 tablespoons natural fromage frais

DAY TWO
BREAKFAST
25 g / 1 oz whole grain cereal of choice with
110 ml / 4 fl oz skimmed milk (extra to allowance) and
25 g / 1 oz chopped apricot mixed in
½ pink grapefruit

LUNCH
Apple, Nut and Carrot Salad
1 crusty brown roll
green salad

EVENING
Spanish Chickpeas
1 banana
3 tablespoons vanilla ice-cream

DAY THREE
BREAKFAST
1 large slice of bread with pure fruit spread
1 kiwi fruit

LUNCH
Pasta Waldorf or 1 pitta bread with 55 g / 2 oz hummus

EVENING
Summer Frittata
65 g / 2½ oz French bread
mixed salad
1 peach with 100 ml / 3½ fl oz low-fat natural yogurt

DAY FOUR
BREAKFAST
3 tablespoons natural fromage frais sprinkled with 15 g / ½ oz *Special Recipe Muesli* and
   1 teaspoon runny honey plus
1 chopped apple

LUNCH
½ portion *Red Lentil Spread* with 65 g / 2½ oz slice of crusty bread
Carrot and Tomato Soup
1 pear

EVENING
Pizza Base topped with *Tomato Sauce*, sliced ½ avocado, and 25 g / 1 oz sliced Mozzarella cheese, baked for 20 minutes
green salad

DAY FIVE
BREAKFAST
1 crusty roll with low-sugar marmalade
1 apple

LUNCH
Cheese and Walnut Dip
2 slices of toast cut into fingers
1 banana

EVENING
Tagliatelle with Wine and Mushrooms
mixed salad
1 piece of fresh fruit or *Marinated Strawberries*

DAY SIX
BREAKFAST
½ portion *Special Recipe Muesli* with
140 ml / 5 fl oz skimmed milk
½ pink grapefruit

LUNCH
50 g / 2 oz rye bread
25 g / 1 oz Brie
Fruit Coleslaw

EVENING
Vegetable Pan-fry
50 g / 2 oz brown and wild rice (dry weight), boiled
1 banana

DAY SEVEN
BREAKFAST
As Day Three

LUNCH
Guacamole with crudités and 2 rye crackers
50 g / 2 oz dried fruit of choice

EVENING
Chinese Egg and Noodle Stir-fry
100 ml / 3½ fl oz Greek-style yogurt
1 teaspoon runny honey

PLAN FOR MEN

This diet will help any man to shed weight painlessly, while at the same time still eating plenty of filling and tasty food.
About 1,500 calories per day

Extras per day: 250 ml / 8 fl oz semi-skimmed milk, 25 g / 1 oz low-fat spread OR 15 g / ½ oz butter or Flora, 1 large glass of wine (optional).

Tagliatelle with wine + mushrooms

DAY ONE
BREAKFAST
Fruit Compote with milk (from allowance)
½ grapefruit

LUNCH
Mushroom Spread (used as a dip) with a selection of crudités
Cantonese Noodle Salad
1 banana

EVENING
Aubergine and Lentil Layer
50 g / 2 oz (dry weight) rice or bulghar, boiled
green salad

DAY TWO
BREAKFAST
American-style Granola with 110 ml / 4 fl oz semi-skimmed milk
1 average slice of bread with reduced sugar marmalade

LUNCH
Curried Lentil and Vegetable Soup
small baguette
1 apple or pear

EVENING
Crispy Vegetable Pie
1 medium portion of lightly cooked greens
1 small portion of mange-tout peas
1 orange

DAY THREE
BREAKFAST
1 average slice of bread
1 large egg, boiled or poached
1 glass of orange juice

LUNCH
Spanish Chickpeas
1 pitta bread

EVENING
Tagliatelle with Wine and Mushrooms
large mixed salad
Baked Peach

DAY FOUR
BREAKFAST
2 medium slices of bread
Apricot Spread
½ grapefruit

LUNCH
one 275 g / 10 oz baked potato filled with *Gumbo Creole*
1 banana

EVENING
Hot and Sour Soup
Bakmie Goreng
3 tablespoons vanilla ice-cream

Hot + Sour soup

DAY FIVE
BREAKFAST
150 g / 5½ oz baked beans on 1 large slice of toast

LUNCH
Pasta Waldorf
1 orange

EVENING
Sultan's Pilaff
yogurt and cucumber salad

DAY SIX
BREAKFAST
as Day Two

LUNCH
Pistou
55 g / 2 oz French bread
1 peach or nectarine

EVENING
Cashew Roast
Tomato Sauce
mixed salad

DAY SEVEN
BREAKFAST
As Day Three

LUNCH
Brown Rice Salad with Mushrooms and Beans
100 g / 3½ oz grapes

EVENING
Chinese Leaf Soup
Chinese Egg and Noodle Stir-fry

FAMILY MENU FOR SLIMMERS

If you like to cook for the family, there is no need to eat separately when you are dieting. This seven-day plan allows for steady weight loss. Non-dieting members of the family can simply eat extra bread, rice, pasta, potatoes, etc – and tuck into extra bakes!
About 1,300 calories per day

Extras per day: 275 ml / 9 fl oz skimmed milk, 15 g / ½ oz low-fat spread, 1 glass of wine (optional).

Classic 3 bean Salad + pasta

DAY ONE
BREAKFAST
1 *Scottish Oatcake* with
    yeast extract
1 glass of orange juice

LUNCH
Classic Three-bean Salad
    with Pasta
green salad

EVENING
Cheese and Onion Bread
    Bake
mixed salad
1 orange

DAY TWO
BREAKFAST
½ portion *Special Recipe*
    Muesli with milk (from
    allowance)
1 apple

LUNCH
Black Bean Soup
1 large slice of bread
1 kiwi fruit
1 slice of *Caribbean Teacake*

EVENING
Polenta with Peppers
Tomato Sauce
mixed salad
Summer Pudding

DAY THREE
BREAKFAST
25 g / 1 oz whole grain cereal
    with milk (from allowance)
1 average slice of bread
    with yeast extract or pure
    fruit spread

LUNCH
Cheese and Walnut Dip in
    1 wholemeal bread roll
tomato and onion salad

EVENING
Cobbler-topped Casserole
1 portion of lightly cooked
    green vegetables of choice
Baked Bananas with Lemon
    and Orange

DAY FOUR
BREAKFAST
1 glass of orange juice
1 large slice bread with
    Apricot Spread

LUNCH
Gado Gado
1 apple

EVENING
Rich Potato Bake
1 portion of baby sweetcorn
1 portion of broccoli

DAY FIVE
BREAKFAST
110 g / 4 oz mushrooms,
    sliced and sautéed in 15 g /
    ½ oz low-fat spread (extra
    to allowance) on
    1 average slice of
    wholemeal toast
½ grapefruit

LUNCH
Pea and Watercress Soup
1 roll
1 large banana

EVENING
Broccoli and Sweetcorn Flan
Fried Peppers with Tomato
    and Garlic
150 g / 5½ oz new potatoes

DAY SIX
BREAKFAST
½ portion of *Fruit Compote*
100 ml / 3½ fl oz low-fat
    natural yogurt

LUNCH
Mexican-style Dip
1 pitta bread
Fruit Coleslaw

EVENING
Sultan's Pilaff
green salad

DAY SEVEN
BREAKFAST
American-style Granola with
    100 ml / 3½ fl oz natural
    fromage frais and 110 g /
    4 oz chopped fresh fruit of
    choice

LUNCH
Pistou
1 large slice of crusty bread

EVENING
Three-bean Casserole
110 g / 4 oz (cooked weight)
    rice or other grain of
    choice
1 large portion of spring
    greens or white cabbage,
    lightly cooked
Baked Peach

TEENAGERS' SLIMMING PLAN

Teenagers need plenty of calories – even if they do need to lose a little weight. This diet will give them all the nutrients they need and won't leave them hungry while they lose weight slowly.
About 1,500 calories per day

Extras per day: 225 ml/7½ fl oz semi-skimmed milk, 15 g/½ oz low-fat spread, 100 calories 'spare' for an extra treat, such as a portion of ice-cream, a glass of lemonade, a fruit bar or a small slice of teabread.

DAY ONE
BREAKFAST
1 *Pineapple Muffin*
200 ml/7 fl oz semi-skimmed milk (extra to allowance)
1 orange

LUNCH
Red Lentil Spread in a bap with plenty of salad
1 large banana

EVENING
Vegetable Pan-fry
1 large slice of bread
Hazelnut Ice-cream

DAY TWO
BREAKFAST
American-style Granola with 140 ml/¼ pint semi-skimmed milk (extra to allowance)
1 glass of orange juice

LUNCH
Pasta Waldorf
1 medium slice of bread
green salad

EVENING
Provençal Pancakes with Cheese Sauce
1 portion of broccoli
Baked Bananas with Lemon and Orange

DAY THREE
BREAKFAST
Cashew Nut Spread on 1 large slice of toast
1 glass of orange juice

LUNCH
Carrot and Tomato Soup
1 bread roll
1 apple
1 *Peach and Raisin Cookie*

EVENING
Tofu and Vegetable Medley
50 g/2 oz (dry weight) egg thread noodles, reconstituted according to packet instructions
1 set fruit yogurt

DAY FOUR
BREAKFAST
Fruit Compote
2 tablespoons Greek yogurt

LUNCH
2 average slices of wholemeal bread filled with 40 g/1½ oz reduced-fat vegetarian Cheddar cheese and pickle
1 orange
1 slice of *Banana and Walnut Teabread*

EVENING
Falafel Patties
1 pitta bread
mixed salad with 1 level tablespoon *Light Mayonnaise*
Summer Pudding with 1 tablespoon fromage frais

DAY FIVE
BREAKFAST
150 g/5½ oz baked beans on 1 large slice of toast
1 orange

LUNCH
Parsley and Potato Soup
1 large bap
1 large banana

EVENING
Pizza Base topped with *Tomato Sauce*, sliced tomatoes and 25 g/1 oz grated Mozzarella cheese, then baked for 20 minutes
1 fruit yogurt
side salad

DAY SIX
BREAKFAST
As Day Two

LUNCH
sandwich of 2 medium slices of bread filled with 2 hard-boiled eggs and plenty of salad
1 apple
1 *Pineapple Muffin*

EVENING
Cashew Roast
Tomato Sauce
large mixed salad with *Oil-free Vinegar Dressing*
100 g/3½ oz (cooked weight) boiled brown rice

DAY SEVEN
BREAKFAST
1 *Reduced-fat Scone* with *Apricot Spread*
1 glass of orange juice

LUNCH
one 225 g/8 oz baked potato with *Lentil Sauce*
1 peach or pear

EVENING
Macaroni, Red Pepper and Broccoli Bake
green salad
1 diet fromage frais

49

Soups, starters and snacks

Soups and starters really are the most versatile of vegetarian dishes – and all the more useful because most are so simple to cook!

Don't think of soups as just winter dishes – at any time of year they can inject variety, taste, nutrition and filling power into a vegetarian diet. They can perform any role, supporting as a light starter or starring as a substantial lunch or supper, hot or cold, quick and easy or more elaborate and impressive.

I have selected a cross-section of soups for all occasions and all tastes – but each is a particular favourite. When you have tried them you will realize that soup-making isn't difficult and you can perhaps invent some variations of your own.

A good stock is essential in most soups. Almost any combination of vegetables – with pulses for a main-meal soup – can be simmered in the stock, and then puréed or left in chunks. Experiment with herbs and spices for extra flavour. For a healthy soup you don't need to sauté the vegetables in oil beforehand, as recipes often suggest. Neither is there any need to garnish or thicken with cream – yogurt or fromage frais will do very well.

The starters I have selected can also be used as light lunches if you are watching your weight. A balanced selection of them could also form the basis of a good buffet or a mezze-type starter for a dinner party.

For other ideas, any of the dips on pages 64–5 will make an informal starter with toast or crudités. Served in half portions, the main-course salads beginning on page 96 will make good starters, as can many other dishes like, say, the Polenta and Peppers on page 74.

Don't forget even simpler starter ideas, like large black stuffed olives, slices of ripe melon, hummus or cucumber and yogurt with crudités, etc. Remember also to balance the meal: for nutrition and appeal, choose a low-calorie, low-fat starter if you have a higher-calorie, higher-fat main course, and vice versa.

HOT AND SOUR SOUP

Perfect to serve before a Thai or Indonesian main course.

Calories per serving: 126
Saturated fat: Medium
Total fat: High
Protein: High
Carbohydrate: Low
Cholesterol: 62.5 mg
Vitamins: A, B, D, C, E
Minerals: Iron, Calcium,
    Potassium

1 litre / 1¾ pints *Vegetable Stock*
    (see page 122)
40 g / 1½ oz cellophane noodles,
    soaked and cut into short pieces
110 g / 4 oz firm tofu, finely chopped
4 Chinese mushrooms, soaked and
    chopped
1 bamboo shoot, chopped
2 medium spring onions, sliced
    lengthwise
1 tsp grated root ginger
1 dsp cornflour mixed with 2 tbsp cold
    water
1 egg, lightly beaten
1 tbsp tomato purée
1 tbsp light soya sauce
1 tbsp vinegar
1 dsp Oriental sesame oil
pinch of chilli powder
salt and black pepper

In a large saucepan bring the stock to the boil.
    Add the noodles, tofu, mushrooms, bamboo shoot, onions, ginger and cornflour mixture. Stir, add the egg and stir again.
    Add the remaining ingredients (you may not want to add any extra salt, so check the taste first before seasoning).

BLACK BEAN SOUP

This is soup is really easy to make, but surprisingly good to taste.

Calories per serving: 156
Saturated fat: Low
Total fat: Low
Protein: High
Carbohydrate: High
Cholesterol: Nil
Vitamins: B group, C
Minerals: Iron, Potassium,
    Calcium

175 g / 6 oz black beans (dry weight),
    soaked as described on pages 22–3
    then drained
825 ml / 1½ pints *Vegetable Stock*
    (see page 122)
1 large onion, chopped
4 celery stalks, chopped
50 g / 2 oz mushrooms, sliced
1 bay leaf
1 clove
1 garlic clove, crushed
1 tsp Tabasco or other hot chilli sauce
1 dsp tomato purée
salt and black pepper

Put the drained beans in a saucepan with all the other ingredients except salt.
    Bring to the boil and boil rapidly for 10 minutes, then reduce the heat and simmer for 1½ hours or until the beans are tender.
    Blend most of the soup in a blender or sieve, then return it to the pan. Taste and add a little salt if required.

CURRIED LENTIL AND VEGETABLE SOUP

This is my second-favourite winter soup after Pistou (see below), and it is so easy you simply can't go wrong with it.

Calories per serving: 220
Saturated fat: Low
Total fat: Medium
Protein: High
Carbohydrate: High
Cholesterol: Nil
Vitamins: C, A, E
Minerals: Iron, Calcium, Potassium

1½ tbsp corn oil
1 level tbsp *Curry Powder* (see recipe on page 122)
1 level tsp ground cumin
1 medium onion, sliced
1.25 litres / 2¼ pints *Vegetable Stock* (see page 122)
1 heaped tbsp tomato purée
125 g / 4½ oz (dry weight) green lentils
110 g / 4 oz broccoli florets
1 medium parsnip, peeled and chopped small
2 medium carrots, peeled and chopped small
1 large celery stalk, chopped
1 tbsp chopped parsley

Heat the oil in heavy-based saucepan and add the curry powder, cumin and onion. Sauté for 5 minutes, stirring frequently.

Pour in the stock, bring to the boil and stir in the tomato purée. Reduce the heat, add the lentils, cover and simmer for 45 minutes, or until the lentils are tender.

Put the rest of the vegetables in the pan, cover and simmer for a further 45 minutes (this may seem longer than necessary, but it produces a tastier, more 'together' soup).

Serve garnished with parsley.

PISTOU

This glorious Provençal soup is a bit of effort to make, but well worth it for a lunch or supper with friends. It is best served with a Mediterranean-style bread to dip in it. This makes it a meal in itself which isn't at all high in fat.

Calories per serving: 235
Saturated fat: Medium
Total fat: High
Protein: High
Carbohydrate: Low
Cholesterol: 11 mg
Vitamins: C, A
Minerals: Potassium, Calcium

1 dsp olive oil
1 medium onion, sliced thinly then chopped
1 litre / 1¾ pints *Vegetable Stock* (see page 122) or water
1 small potato (about 110 g / 4 oz), diced
2 medium carrots, peeled and diced
2 celery stalks, chopped
25 g / 1 oz (dry weight) pasta shapes
110 g / 4 oz French beans, trimmed and cut in half
2 medium courgettes (about 225 g / 8 oz in total), sliced
125 g / 4½ oz (cooked weight) green flageolet beans (canned will do)
salt
for the red pesto sauce:
2 large garlic cloves
15 g / ½ oz fresh basil
50 g / 2 oz grated vegetarian Parmesan cheese
2 medium tomatoes or 1 beef tomato, skinned, deseeded and chopped
2 dsp olive oil

Heat the oil in a heavy-based saucepan, add the onion and stir for a few minutes until soft.

Pour in the stock or water and bring to the boil. Reduce the heat and add the potato, carrots and celery. Cover and simmer for 10 minutes.

Add the pasta, French beans and courgettes and cook, uncovered, for 10 minutes. Add the flageolets and simmer for 5 minutes. Taste the soup and add a pinch of salt if necessary.

Meanwhile, make the sauce: in a mortar, pound the garlic and basil together with a little salt until you have a paste. Add the grated cheese and chopped tomato, each a little at a time, pounding thoroughly until you have a thicker paste. Finally, work in the olive oil until you have a rich thick sauce.

Put the sauce in a bowl and hand it round with a spoon for guests to help themselves. The sauce is best dolloped in the middle of the soup, where it will gradually dissolve and give the classic pistou aroma and flavour.

CARROT AND TOMATO SOUP

I find most carrot soups too sweet and bland for my taste, but this has a nice tart bite to it.

Calories per serving: 86
Saturated fat: High
Total fat: High
Protein: Medium
Carbohydrate: Medium
Cholesterol: 3.5 mg
Vitamins: A, C, E
Minerals: Potassium

1 tbsp sunflower oil
175 g / 6 oz carrots, peeled and chopped
1 garlic clove, chopped
1 medium onion, finely chopped
225 g / 8 oz fresh tasty tomatoes, skinned and chopped
1 level tsp ground cumin
425 ml / ¾ pint *Vegetable Stock* (see page 122)
bouquet garni
bay leaf
1 tbsp dry sherry
4 tbsp thick single cream
salt (optional)

Heat the oil in a heavy-based saucepan, add the carrot, garlic and onion and sweat over a low heat for 10 minutes.

Add the tomatoes and cumin, cover and simmer 2 minutes. Add the stock and herbs and simmer for 15 minutes more.

Remove the herbs and put the soup through a blender. Return to the pan, stir in the sherry and reheat. Taste and add a little salt if wished.

Swirl in the cream to serve.

Note: this soup does benefit from the little bit of cream, but if you want to save a little fat and about 12 calories per serving you could add some 0%-fat fromage frais instead or simply leave the cream out and garnish with chopped parsley.

PEA AND WATERCRESS SOUP

This soup is just as good served cold as hot. For a change, try shredding some lettuce and adding it to the soup while it reheats.

Calories per serving: 93
Saturated fat: Low
Total fat: Medium
Protein: High
Carbohydrate: High
Cholesterol: Nil
Vitamins: C, A, E, B group
Minerals: Potassium, Iron, Calcium

15 g / 1½ oz low-fat spread
1 medium onion, chopped
825 ml / 1½ pints *Vegetable Stock* (see page 122)
325 g / 12 oz tender frozen peas
1 good bunch of watercress, trimmed, washed and chopped
2 tbsp chopped fresh mint
salt and black pepper

Melt the fat in a heavy-based saucepan and sauté the onion until soft.

Add the stock, peas and watercress. Bring to the boil, then simmer for 10 minutes.

Season to taste and put the soup through the blender. Return to the pan, add the mint and heat through to serve.

Note: you can add a dash of single cream or fromage frais to each dish before serving, which would add only a very few extra calories.

OPPOSITE: Carrot and Tomato Soup; Pea and Watercress Soup

PARSLEY AND POTATO SOUP

A friend gave me this recipe – for which I am very grateful, as I would never have thought the strong taste of parsley would turn into such a brilliantly subtle flavour in this soup. However, it does, and the soup is also very rich in vitamins and minerals.

Calories per serving: 154
Saturated fat: Medium
Total fat: Medium
Protein: Medium
Carbohydrate: High
Cholesterol: 4.5 mg
Vitamins: A, C, B, E,
Minerals: Potassium, Iron,
 Calcium

1 dsp olive oil
small knob of butter
1 medium onion, finely chopped
2 garlic cloves, chopped
350 g / 12½ oz potato, peeled and
 diced
550 ml / 1 pint *Vegetable Stock*
 (see page 122)
250 ml / ½ pint skimmed milk
50 g / 2 oz very fresh parsley, trimmed
 and chopped
salt and black pepper

Heat the oil and butter in a heavy-based saucepan and sauté the onion and garlic for 5 minutes, or until soft and just turning golden.

   Add the potato and stir. Sweat the contents of the pan over a low heat for 10 minutes. Add the stock and milk and bring to the boil. Reduce the heat and simmer until all the vegetables are soft (about 15 minutes).

   Add the parsley and simmer for a further 5 minutes. Add some black pepper to taste.

   Put the soup through a blender, then add salt to taste and serve.

CHINESE LEAF SOUP

This soup is so delicious, no one but the chef will ever realize just how easy it is to prepare.

Calories per serving: 92
Saturated fat: Low
Total fat: Medium
Protein: High
Carbohydrate: High
Cholesterol: 12 mg
Vitamins: A, C, B group
Minerals: Calcium, Potassium,
 Iron

50 g / 2 oz dried egg-thread noodles
1 dsp sunflower or corn oil
1 large garlic clove, chopped and
 crushed
825 ml / 1½ pints *Vegetable Stock*
 (see page 122)
175 g / 6 oz Chinese leaves, thinly
 sliced
1 tbsp light soy sauce
100 g / 3½ oz fresh beansprouts
pinch of sugar
1 tbsp chopped fresh coriander
pinch of chilli powder

Soak the noodles until soft as per packet instructions. Drain, separate and chop into short pieces.

   Heat the oil in a non-stick frying pan or wok over a medium heat and stir the garlic in it for a minute. Add the stock and bring to the boil.

   Add the Chinese leaves and simmer for 2 minutes. Add the soy sauce, beansprouts, prepared noodles and the sugar. Stir and heat through.

   Add the coriander and chilli powder to garnish and serve.

LEEK AND CHIVE SOUP

This soup proves that there is absolutely no need to use cream in soups to obtain a gorgeous creamy taste and texture.

Calories per serving: 160
Saturated fat: Medium
Total fat: Medium
Protein: High
Carbohydrate: High
Cholesterol: 9 mg
Vitamins: C
Minerals: Iron, Potassium, Calcium

4 large leeks (about 650 g / 1½ lb in total)
15 g / ½ oz butter
2 medium potatoes (about 225 g / 8 oz), peeled and diced
1 medium onion, chopped
825 ml / 1½ pints *Vegetable Stock* (see page 122)
250 ml / ½ pint skimmed milk
3 tbsp chopped fresh chives
salt and black pepper

Trim the leeks, discarding only the dark green part of the leaves and the tough bases. Split the trimmed leeks in half lengthwise and then chop them small. Wash thoroughly in cold water and drain.

In a large heavy-based saucepan or flameproof casserole, gently melt the butter. Add the drained leeks, the potatoes and onion. Stir, cover and sweat over a low heat for 10 minutes.

Add the stock and milk, bring to the boil and simmer gently for 20 minutes. Allow to cool a little.

Add 1 tablespoon of the chives and blend thoroughly in an electric blender. Return to the pan and reheat.

Season and serve garnished with the remaining chives.

Note: this recipe can be adapted to make a stunning creamed broccoli soup: simply substitute 500 g / 18 oz broccoli florets for the leeks, use 550 ml / 1 pint skimmed milk and only 550 ml / 1 pint Vegetable Stock. Calorie and nutrition details are similar. You may omit the chives and add a pinch of nutmeg instead.

ITALIAN ARTICHOKES

This dish makes a superb starter before a high-carbohydrate Italian main dish such as pasta or risotto. A half-portion with some crusty Ciabatta would make a light summer lunch.

Calories per serving: 95
Saturated fat: Medium
Total fat: High
Protein: Medium
Carbohydrate: Low
Cholesterol: Nil
Vitamins: E
Minerals: Trace

400 g / 14 oz can of artichoke hearts (8 whole hearts), drained
2 canned red peppers or piquillos, drained (or use fresh peppers, skinned and thinly sliced)
3 tbsp sunflower oil
2 tbsp extra virgin olive oil
1 tbsp white wine vinegar
1 garlic clove, crushed
1 tsp chopped chervil
1 tbsp chopped parsley
salt and black pepper

Rinse the artichokes thoroughly in cold water, pat dry on paper towels and cut in halves. Place these in a bowl with the pepper strips.

Combine the remaining ingredients well (you could use a blender but, in that case, add the chervil and parsley after blending), season to taste and toss with the artichokes. Cover and refrigerate for an hour or two.

Serve the artichokes on individual plates with a little of the dressing spooned over.

Note: fine green beans make a nice alternative to the peppers.

MARINATED MUSHROOMS WITH CORIANDER

Serve fresh crusty French bread to mop up the moreish sauce.

Calories per serving: 50
Saturated fat: Medium
Total fat: High
Protein: Medium
Carbohydrate: Low
Cholesterol: Nil
Vitamins: C, A, E
Minerals: Potassium

325 g / 12 oz button mushrooms
3 tbsp white wine vinegar
1 tbsp lemon juice
1 tbsp olive oil
1 garlic clove, chopped
1 small bay leaf
pinch of brown sugar
1 level tsp ground coriander seeds
100 ml / 3½ fl oz passata
salt and black pepper
2 tbsp chopped parsley or coriander

Brush the mushrooms clean, if necessary, and place them in a bowl.

Put all the remaining ingredients except the chopped fresh herbs in a small pan, season well and bring to the boil, stirring. Simmer for 2 minutes.

Pour this over the mushrooms and leave to marinate for several hours, overnight if possible.

Serve cold or reheated, with the chopped herbs sprinkled over.

MARINATED AUBERGINE AND TOMATO

Nothing could be simpler than this starter, which could also be used as a side vegetable.

Calories per serving: 90
Saturated fat: Medium
Total fat: High
Protein: Medium
Carbohydrate: Low
Cholesterol: Nil
Vitamins: A, C, E
Minerals: Potassium

3 tbsp balsamic vinegar
2 tbsp olive oil
2 garlic cloves, crushed
2 small aubergines
2 beef tomatoes
black pepper
2 tbsp fresh chopped basil

Preheat a medium grill.

Make a dressing by mixing together the vinegar, olive oil, garlic and pepper. Top and tail the aubergines, cut into rounds about 1 cm / ½ in thick and brush with half the dressing.

Grill until golden on both sides, turning once (about 3 minutes per side).

Slice the tomatoes horizontally into rounds and arrange on a serving dish (or individual dishes) with the cooked aubergine slices. Pour the remaining dressing over and leave to marinate for an hour or two.

Just before serving, sprinkle over the basil.

CROSTINI

These traditional little Italian snacks also make ideal buffet fare, or a light lunch in themselves if you're watching the calories.

Calories per serving: 126
Saturated fat: Medium
Total fat: Medium
Protein: Medium
Carbohydrate: Medium
Cholesterol: 3.5 mg
Vitamins: A, C, E, Folic acid
Minerals: Potassium, Calcium

1 medium aubergine
1 tbsp olive oil
1 medium Spanish onion, finely
    chopped
1 large garlic clove, crushed
100 g / 3½ oz mushrooms, sliced
4 stoned green olives, chopped
200 g / 7 oz canned chopped
    tomatoes, drained
25 g / 1 oz Italian buffalo Mozzarella,
    diced
1 tsp chopped fresh or dried basil
4 medium-thick slices of Ciabatta
    bread
salt and black pepper

Preheat a medium hot oven (190°C / 375°F / gas5). Bake the aubergines in the oven until tender (about 45 minutes). Let cool slightly, then halve and scoop out the flesh.

Meanwhile, heat the oil in a non-stick frying pan and sauté the onion and garlic until soft, stirring frequently. When they are just turning golden, add the mushrooms and stir for 3 minutes.

Add the aubergine flesh to the pan with the seasonings, olives, tomatoes and cheese. Stir and simmer for 5 minutes.

Toast the bread and top with the mixture. Cut into fingers or triangles to serve.

OPPOSITE: Marinated Mushrooms with Coriander; Marinated Aubergine and Tomato

MIXED PEPPER CROUSTADES

You need four large bun tins or individual flan tins for this recipe.

Calories per serving: 128
Saturated fat: Low
Total fat: High
Protein: Medium
Carbohydrate: High
Cholesterol: Nil
Vitamins: A, C, E
Minerals: Potassium, Iron

1 tbsp olive oil, plus more for brushing
4 thin slices of bread, cut into
    9 cm / 3½ in rounds
1 small onion, sliced
275 g / 10 oz mixed peppers (including
    at least one red), deseeded and
    chopped into diamonds
1 garlic clove, chopped
200 g / 7 oz canned chopped
    tomatoes, drained
1 tsp chopped fresh or dried basil
salt and black pepper
black olives, halved, to garnish

Preheat the oven to 180°C / 350°F / gas4.

Brush the tins lightly with olive oil and press the bread slices into the tins. Brush the bread lightly with oil and bake for 10 minutes until pale golden.

Meanwhile, heat the tablespoon of oil in a non-stick frying pan and sauté the onion and peppers for 20 minutes, stirring frequently, until they are very soft and golden at the edges. Add the garlic and stir for a minute. Add the tomatoes, herbs and seasoning and stir for 3 minutes.

Spoon the pepper mixture into the croustades and serve, garnished with olives.

LENTIL PATE

This tasty and satisfying pâté is simple to make and can be adapted for use as a spread or a dip by adding more stock.

Calories per serving: 48
Saturated fat: Low
Total fat: Low
Protein: High
Carbohydrate: High
Cholesterol: Nil
Vitamins: B group
Minerals: Iron, Magnesium,
    Potassium, Zinc

250 ml / ½ pint *Vegetable Stock*
    (see page 122)
50 g / 2 oz (dry weight) Puy lentils
2 spring onions, finely chopped
1 tbsp freshly chopped sage
salt and black pepper
more sage leaves, to garnish

Put the stock in a saucepan and add the lentils, bring to a simmer and cook the lentils until tender – about 30 minutes.

In an electric blender, blend the cooked lentils and stock together with the spring onions and chopped sage. Season to taste.

Spoon into 4 small containers and garnish with sage leaves.

PIQUILLO CREAMS

These are delicious served with crusty bread or toast.

Calories per serving: 58
Saturated fat: Medium
Total fat: Medium
Protein: Medium
Carbohydrate: High
Cholesterol: 5 mg
Vitamins: A, C, E
Minerals: Calcium

6 canned piquillos (Spanish red
    peppers), drained and chopped
100 g / 3½ oz low-fat natural fromage
    frais
50 g / 2 oz low-fat soft cheese
1 tsp garlic paste
pinch of chilli powder (optional)
little black pepper
2 tsp balsamic vinegar
2 tbsp very hot water
1 sachet of agar-agar
watercress, to garnish

Purée the peppers, cheeses, garlic paste, chilli powder if using, black pepper and vinegar in a blender.

Put the hot water in a small heatproof bowl. Sprinkle the agar-agar into it and stir until dissolved. Add this to the pepper mixture and stir thoroughly.

Divide the mixture between 4 ramekins and chill until set.

Serve in the dishes or turned out on plates, garnished with watercress.

OPPOSITE: Mixed Pepper Croustades

Dips, spreads and sauces

These easy-to-make dips, spreads and sauces are an indispensable part of the healthy vegetarian diet as they are perfect for snacks and quick meals.

I've combined dips, spreads and sauces because many are versatile enough to be interchangeable. By my definition a 'spread' should be eaten cold and be thin enough to spread easily, but thick enough to stay put when sandwiched. A 'dip' is normally eaten cold, thinner and served in a container in which you dip crudités, etc. A 'sauce' may be hot or cold and will pour.

I have chosen to categorize the recipes that follow as dips or spreads or sauces, but many can be slightly adapted to turn one into something else! A dip can often be thickened, either by reducing the quantity of liquid in it or by adding breadcrumbs, to make a spread. You can also thicken a savoury spread (eg the Mushroom Spread on page 66) with breadcrumbs and turn it into a pâté to use as a starter. The spreads can usually be thinned down with stock, milk or water to make a dip. The dips may be thinned in the same ways to make sauces. The cooked sauces can be reduced to a dip by simmering them gently until thickened.

Suggestions for using the dips and spreads within your diet appear in the plans on pages 35–9 and 45–9. Most of the sauces are used within other recipes but here are some more guidelines on using them. The Tomato Sauce you will use frequently to top pasta or pizza, to add moisture and flavour to bakes, or as the basis of soups and casseroles. Make plenty and freeze it. You can vary the basic recipe with added herbs, chilli, mushrooms or garlic. The Mediterranean and Lentil Sauces are ideal for pasta, rice or baked potatoes, or with eggs. The Cheese Sauce is used in Mornays, lasagnes, moussakas, bakes and with eggs, spinach and grains. The Sweet-and-sour is a good sauce to add to all stir-fries, and the Fresh Tomato Salsa is perfect with loaves and patties, as a dipping sauce or in all Mexican dishes.

Top: Tomato Sauce (page 69); bottom: Sweet-and-sour Sauce (page 66)
served on Pancakes (page 121) filled with asparagus

AVOCADO AND TOFU DIP

Calories per serving: 110
Saturated fat: Medium
Total fat: High
Protein: Medium
Carbohydrate: Low
Cholesterol: Nil
Vitamins: E, C, Folic acid
Minerals: Potassium,
*   Magnesium, Calcium, Iron*

1 large ripe avocado
2 tsp lemon juice
125 g / 4½ oz silken tofu
2 tsp chopped spring onions
1 level tsp Tabasco sauce
salt

Peel, stone and chop the avocado and toss it with the lemon juice in a blender goblet. Add the rest of the ingredients, with salt to taste and blend until smooth.
Note: this makes a good topping for baked potatoes, as well as being a fine dip or spread for crackers.

CHEESE AND WALNUT DIP

Like most nuts, walnuts are high in fat – so the secret is to use them in moderation for added taste and bite. They are also a good source of minerals.

Calories per serving: 117
Saturated fat: High
Total fat: High
Protein: High
Carbohydrate: Low
Cholesterol: 6 mg
Vitamins A, C, Folic acid
Minerals: Calcium, Iron,
*   Magnesium*

175 g / 6 oz natural diet cottage
    cheese
1 heaped tbsp grated vegetarian
    Parmesan cheese
1 tbsp olive oil
3 tbsp skimmed milk
2 tbsp spring onions
1 tbsp parsley
25 g / 1 oz chopped walnuts
salt and black pepper

Blend the cheeses, oil and seasonings. Add just enough skimmed milk to make a softish consistency.

Add the onions, parsley and walnuts and stir in well.

MEXICAN-STYLE DIP

Good with corn chips, crispbread or on hot toast, garnished with chopped cucumber.

Calories per serving: 105
Saturated fat: Medium
Total fat: High
Protein: High
Carbohydrate: Medium
Cholesterol: 1 mg
Vitamins: C, E, B group
Minerals: Calcium, Potassium,
*   Magnesium, Iron*

1 tbsp olive oil
425 g / 15 oz canned red kidney
    beans, drained (reserving liquid),
    or 275 g / 10 oz pre-cooked red
    kidney beans plus some of the
    cooking water .
1 small green pepper, deseeded and
    chopped
salt
1 level tsp chilli powder
1 level tbsp grated Pecorino cheese
thick rounds of cucumber, to serve
    (optional)

Heat the oil in a heavy-based saucepan and add all the ingredients except the cheese, together with a little chilli powder to taste.

Cook over medium heat for 15 minutes, adding a little reserved bean liquid as necessary to give a medium-textured dip. Taste and add more chilli powder if necessary.

Serve hot or cold on rounds of cucumber, if using, topped with the cheese.

GUACAMOLE

Calories per serving: 116
Saturated fat: Low
Total fat: High
Protein: Medium
Carbohydrate: Low
Cholesterol: Nil
Vitamins: E, C, A
Minerals: Potassium, Iron

1 large ripe avocado
1 tbsp fresh lime juice
1 medium tomato, skinned and
    chopped
1 small garlic clove, crushed
2 spring onions, chopped
pinch of chilli powder
salt and black pepper

Skin and stone the avocado quickly and chop the flesh into a bowl. Quickly mix with the lime juice. Mash together with the rest of the ingredients and season to taste.

Serve with tortilla chips for a change.
Note: the mixture can also be used to stuff beef tomatoes. Bake for 10 minutes in a moderately hot oven or microwave on HIGH for 1 minute each tomato.

ABOVE: Guacamole

65

RED LENTIL SPREAD

Calories per serving: 133
Saturated fat: Low
Total fat: Medium
Protein: High
Carbohydrate: Medium
Cholesterol: Nil
Vitamins: B group
Minerals: Iron, Potassium,
*   Magnesium, Zinc*

100 g / 3½ oz red lentils
10 g / ⅓ oz polyunsaturated margarine
1 tbsp olive oil
1 tbsp tomato purée
little lemon juice
salt and pepper

Simmer the lentils in 200 ml / 7 fl oz water until very soft – about 45 minutes.

Mash them together with any remaining water in the pan and the rest of the ingredients, adding lemon juice and seasoning to taste.

CASHEW NUT SPREAD

Calories per serving: 130
Saturated fat: Medium
Total fat: High
Protein: Medium
Carbohydrate: Low
Cholesterol: Nil
Vitamins: Folic acid, C
Minerals: Calcium, Iron,
*   Potassium*

1 dsp olive oil
1 small onion, finely chopped
1 small garlic clove, crushed
65 g / 2½ oz toasted cashew nuts, ground
125 g / 4½ oz silken tofu
1 tbsp chopped parsley
salt

Heat the oil in a small heavy-based frying pan and sauté the onion until soft, adding the garlic for the last minute or two.

Add the onion and garlic to the nuts in a mixing bowl. Add all the remaining ingredients with 3 tablespoons of water and mix together well. Taste and adjust the seasoning, if necessary.

MUSHROOM SPREAD

Calories per serving: 65
Saturated fat: High
Total fat: High
Protein: Medium
Carbohydrate: Low
Cholesterol: Nil
Vitamins: C, B group
Minerals: Calcium

1 tbsp olive oil
1 small onion, finely chopped
175 g / 6 oz tasty mushrooms, sliced
1 small garlic clove, crushed
25 g / 1 oz brown breadcrumbs
50 g / 2 oz 0%-fat fromage frais
1 dsp soy sauce
1 tsp lemon juice
pinch of freshly grated nutmeg
pinch of paprika

Heat the oil in a heavy-based saucepan and sauté the onion until soft. Add the mushrooms and garlic and sauté again for a few minutes, stirring continuously.

Transfer to a blender, add all the remaining ingredients and blend until smooth.

SWEET-AND-SOUR SAUCE

This is a good stand-by to add to stir-fries.

Calories per serving: 26
Saturated fat: Nil
Total fat: Low
Protein: Medium
Carbohydrate: High
Cholesterol: Nil
Vitamins: C
Minerals: Trace

2 tbsp dark soy sauce
about ½ tsp chilli sauce
2 tbsp tomato purée
2 tbsp red wine vinegar
about 2 level tsp sugar
1 heaped tsp cornflour
150 ml / 5½ fl oz *Vegetable Stock* (see page 122) or water

Put all the ingredients in a small saucepan. Place over medium heat, stirring all the time, until the sauce thickens. Simmer for a few minutes.

Adjust the flavour with a little more chilli sauce to get the favoured degree of hotness, and a little more sugar or vinegar to get the right sweet-and-sour balance for your taste.

FRESH TOMATO SALSA

The refreshing taste of this sauce goes well with many dishes, such as polenta and nut loaves, and it makes a good topping for pancakes, omelettes or tacos.

Calories per serving: 25
Saturated fat: Low
Total fat: Low
Protein: High
Carbohydrate: High
Cholesterol: Nil
Vitamins: A, C
Minerals: Potassium

2 beef tomatoes, skinned and
  chopped
1 red pepper, deseeded and chopped
1 fresh chilli, deseeded and chopped
salt and black pepper

Put all the ingredients in a blender and blend until you have a sauce which still has some texture to it – ie, don't over-blend.
Notes: you can add extra flavourings to this sauce to suit your own taste: eg a small amount of fresh garlic, a dash of wine vinegar for more piquancy or balsamic vinegar for more depth.
Mixed with beans (eg kidney beans) and served with a cooked grain, such as bulghar or rice, this salsa makes a meal in itself.

CHEESE SAUCE

This cheese sauce is a lot lower in fat than the usual cheese sauces.

Calories per serving: 110
Saturated fat: High
Total fat: High
Protein: High
Carbohydrate: Low
Cholesterol: 6 mg
Vitamins: B group, A, D
Minerals: Calcium

25 g / 1 oz low-fat spread
25 g / 1 oz plain white flour
350 ml / 12½ fl oz skimmed milk
65 g / 2½ oz vegetarian low-fat
  Cheddar cheese
1 tsp English mustard powder
  (optional)
salt and pepper

Melt the low-fat spread in a small non-stick saucepan and add the flour off the heat, stirring well. Return to the pan and cook for a minute, stirring, over a medium heat.

Remove from the heat and add a little milk, stirring to form a thick sauce. Put back on the heat and gradually add the remaining milk, stirring constantly, until you have a smooth white sauce.

Add the cheese and mustard, if using, and stir until the cheese melts in. Taste and adjust the seasoning, if necessary.

MEDITERRANEAN SAUCE

One of my very favourite sauces, it is good for pasta, pancakes or in bakes. It also makes a good pizza topping.

Calories per serving: 80
Saturated fat: Medium
Total fat: High
Protein: Medium
Carbohydrate: High
Cholesterol: Nil
Vitamins: A, C, E, Folic acid
Minerals: Potassium

1 medium aubergine
1 tbsp olive oil
1½ large onions, sliced thinly then
  chopped
2 garlic cloves, crushed
100 ml / 3½ fl oz passata
one 400 g / 14 oz can chopped
  tomatoes (with liquid)
8 stoned black olives, chopped
1 dsp chopped basil
salt and black pepper

Top and tail the aubergine and cut it into *small* cubes. Put in a colander, sprinkle with salt and leave for 30 minutes. Rinse and pat dry.

Heat the olive oil in a non-stick frying pan and sauté the onion in it until soft, adding the garlic for the last few minutes.

Add the aubergine cubes, cover and simmer very gently for 20 minutes, adding a little passata if it looks very dry at any time.

Add the tomatoes, olives, basil, remaining passata and seasoning. Simmer, uncovered, for 15 minutes, stirring occasionally. Add extra water at any time as necessary. The sauce should be thick but not too dry.

SPINACH SAUCE

Calories per serving: 53
Saturated fat: Low
Total fat: Low
Protein: High
Carbohydrate: Low
Cholesterol: Nil
Vitamins: A, C, E, Folic acid
Minerals: Calcium, Iron,
  Potassium

450 g / 1 lb fresh spinach, washed
1 garlic clove, crushed
pinch of ground ginger
150 ml / 5½ fl oz low-fat natural
  yogurt
salt

Put the spinach in a saucepan and heat until it wilts.

Drain and liquidize with the rest of ingredients.

Taste and adjust the seasoning, if necessary, before serving with poached eggs or pasta.

TOMATO SAUCE

This is a reduced-fat version of the classic tomato sauce. See note for some variations.

Calories per serving: 60
Saturated fat: Medium
Total fat: High
Protein: Medium
Carbohydrate: Low
Cholesterol: Nil
Vitamins: A, C
Minerals: Iron, Potassium

1 tbsp olive oil
1 medium onion, finely chopped
1 big garlic clove, chopped
425 g / 15 oz ripe tomatoes, skinned
  and chopped, *or* one 400 g / 14 oz
  can chopped tomatoes (with liquid)
1 dsp chopped parsley
1 tbsp tomato purée
1 level tsp brown sugar
1 dsp lemon juice
1 bay leaf
1 dsp chopped basil
tomato juice as required
salt and black pepper

Heat the oil in a heavy-based non-stick pan and sauté the onion gently until very soft, adding the garlic towards the end of this time.

Add the rest of the ingredients, except the basil and tomato juice. Simmer for 30 minutes, uncovered. Remove the bay and add the basil.

If the sauce is too thick for your needs, thin it down with a little tomato juice or passata. Taste and adjust the seasoning, if necessary. *Note*: instead of the basil you can flavour this sauce with many other herbs, such as oregano or tarragon; or try adding some fresh green chillies or half a can of red peppers at the beginning of simmering time.

LENTIL SAUCE

Calories per serving: 204
Saturated fat: Low
Total fat: Low
Protein: High
Carbohydrate: High
Cholesterol: Nil
Vitamins: B group, C, A
Minerals: Iron, Potassium,
  Magnesium, Zinc

175 g / 6 oz red lentils
425 ml / ¾ pint *Vegetable Stock*
  (see page 122) or water
1 dsp olive oil
1 medium onion, finely chopped
1 garlic clove, chopped
one 400 g / 14 oz can chopped
  tomatoes (with liquid)
25 ml / 1 fl oz red wine
1 tbsp lemon juice
1 level tsp five-spice powder

Simmer the lentils in the stock or water until they are very soft (about 45 minutes).

Meanwhile, heat the oil in a medium heavy-based non-stick saucepan and stir-fry the onion for a few minutes until soft, adding a dash of water if it gets too dry.

Add the garlic and stir that for a minute. Add the rest of the ingredients, including the lentil mixture. Simmer for 15 minutes.

Put through the blender, or leave unblended for a coarser sauce. Ideal over pasta.

OPPOSITE: Spinach Sauce on pasta

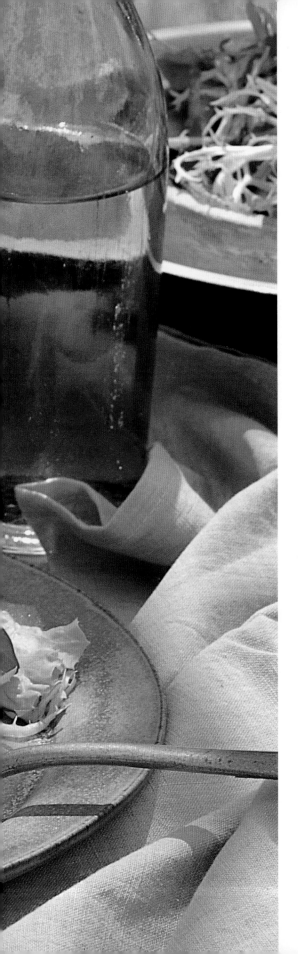

Quick suppers and lunches

When time is short, or if you are eating alone, you'll want something that takes little time to prepare and cook. Here are some of my favourites.

What is the difference between a lunch or supper and a 'main meal'? I suppose a main meal consists of more than one dish – or perhaps just one dish consisting of several component parts. It is also, perhaps, a more formal affair. So the recipes in this chapter are all quick, informal and easy – usually cooked, and sometimes served, in one dish. You'll find more simple healthy ideas for busy days and hungry people in the plans on pages 35–9 and 45–9.

Cold lunch or supper can be as nutritious as a hot dish. Try a large hunk of rye bread with low-fat cheese and tomatoes or apples? Or *pan bagna* – a big baguette filled with salad, olives and hard-boiled egg and drizzled with Light Vinaigrette?

If you have a microwave, potatoes can be baked in minutes and topped with fromage frais mixed with mustard or cooked beans in a ready-made chilli sauce.

Stir-fries can take a lot of preparation (all that chopping and slicing!) but if you pick baby vegetables or legumes little or no preparation is necessary. Mix in some instant soaked noodles or ready-cooked rice and chopped nuts for a quick treat.

Noodles are also a good – almost-instant – base for sauces, as is pasta. If you have a freezer, you can cook up a batch of sauces from the previous chapter and freeze them ready to defrost. Pasta can also be topped even more simply, with garlic or black olives and olive oil, or grated Parmesan and chopped herbs.

Pancakes always make a delicious quick supper, and can be batch-cooked and frozen. Low-fat cheese, such as Feta or Mozzarella, can be arranged with slices of tomato and herbs and melted in the microwave for a quick lunch. If you eat eggs, it is easy to make a herb omelette and serve it with bread and salad.

Remember that fast cooking retains more of the food's nutrients and so is doing you good as well as tasting delicious.

Summer Frittata (page 77) and green salad

SULTAN'S PILAFF

Calories per serving: 520
Saturated fat: Low
Total fat: Medium
Protein: Medium
Carbohydrate: High
Cholesterol: 195 mg
Vitamins: B group, A, D, E
Minerals: Iron, Calcium,
    Magnesium, Zinc, Potassium

15 g / ½ oz low-fat spread
1 tbsp olive oil
325 g / 12 oz Basmati rice, rinsed
700 ml / 1¼ pints *Vegetable Stock*
  (see page 122)
1 level tsp turmeric
50 g / 2 oz pine nuts
75 g / 3 oz (drained weight) canned
  chickpeas
3 hard-boiled eggs, quartered
salt and black pepper

Melt the spread with the oil in a heavy-based pan or flameproof casserole. Add the rice and sauté it, stirring from time to time, over a moderate heat for 2 minutes.

Add the stock and the rest of ingredients, except the eggs. Bring to the boil. Reduce the heat, cover and simmer for 20 minutes, or until the rice is cooked.

Serve garnished with the eggs.

VEGETABLE PAELLA

Be sure to use the best quality saffron you can find for this dish.

Calories per serving: 460
Saturated fat: Medium
Total fat: Low
Protein: Medium
Carbohydrate: High
Cholesterol: 15 mg
Vitamins: A, C, E
Minerals: Potassium, Zinc

1 tbsp olive oil
25 g / 1 oz butter
2 medium onions, chopped
2 garlic cloves, crushed
1 medium leek, thinly sliced
1 medium aubergine, chopped
1 green pepper, deseeded and sliced
50 g / 2 oz petits pois
325 g / 12 oz long-grain rice
1 beef tomato, skinned and chopped
825 ml / 1½ pints *Vegetable Stock*
  (see page 122)
1 or 2 sachets of saffron strands
salt and black pepper

Heat the oil and butter in a large paella pan and sauté the onions and garlic for 4 minutes. Add the rest of the vegetables, except the tomato, and sauté for a few minutes more, stirring well.

Lower the heat and add the rice. Stir again, then add the tomato, stock and saffron and seasonings. Bring to the boil, reduce the heat and simmer until the rice is tender (about 15 minutes), adding extra stock as needed.

Note: 50 g / 2 oz pine nuts added towards the end of cooking time makes this dish even nicer, but will add 70 calories per portion and raise the total fat content to Medium.

SPANISH CHICKPEAS

These are incredibly moreish, but luckily the dish is very good for you and even a double serving wouldn't do too much damage to your diet!

Calories per serving: 266
Saturated fat: Medium
Total fat: Medium
Protein: High
Carbohydrate: High
Cholesterol: 8 mg
Vitamins: A, B group, C, E
Minerals: Iron, Potassium,
  Calcium, Magnesium

15 g / ½ oz butter
1 tbsp olive oil
1 medium onion, chopped
1 garlic clove, crushed
1 green pepper, deseeded and sliced
275 g / 10 oz (drained weight) canned
  chickpeas
175 g / 6 oz sweetcorn
175 g / 6 oz (drained weight) canned
  red kidney beans
½ tsp oregano
1 tsp ground cumin
one 400 g / 14 oz can chopped
  tomatoes (with liquid)
2 fresh green chillies, deseeded and
  chopped
salt

Heat the butter and oil in heavy-based frying pan and sauté the onion, garlic and green pepper until soft.

Add the rest of the ingredients, cover and cook for 20 minutes or more.

Serve very hot.

SOUFFLE POTATOES

This makes a nice change from the baked potato.

Calories per serving: 205
Saturated fat: Low
Total fat: Medium
Protein: Medium
Carbohydrate: High
Cholesterol: 63 mg
Vitamins: C
Minerals: Potassium

2 large baking potatoes, scrubbed
1 tbsp skimmed milk
1 egg, separated
15 g / ½ oz low-fat spread
1 level tbsp grated Parmesan cheese
salt and black pepper

Preheat the oven to 200°C / 400°F / gas6.

Prick the potatoes and put metal skewers through the middle of both. Bake for 1 hour, until the insides are very tender.

Cool slightly, then cut in half. Scoop out the flesh carefully and mash it with the milk, egg yolk, low-fat spread, cheese and seasoning.

Whisk the egg white until stiff and fold this into the potato mixture. Fill each potato skin with the mixture and return to the oven for 10 minutes, or until risen and lightly browned.

VEGETABLE PAN-FRY

Try cooking this versatile mixture as one flat cake.

Calories per serving: 235
Saturated fat: Low
Total fat: High
Protein: Medium
Carbohydrate: High
Cholesterol: 125 mg
Vitamins: C, A, B group
Minerals: Potassium, Iron

275 g / 10 oz leeks
275 g / 10 oz carrots, grated
325 g / 12 oz potatoes, grated
1 medium onion, finely chopped
2 garlic cloves, finely chopped
bunch of parsley, finely chopped
2 medium eggs
110 g / 4 oz breadcrumbs
salt and black pepper
1 dsp corn oil

Trim the leeks, halve them and cut them into thin slices. Rinse, drain and dry well on paper towels. Also dry the grated carrots and potatoes on paper towels.

Put all these vegetables in a big bowl with the onion, garlic, parsley, eggs, breadcrumbs and seasoning and mix well. Leave to stand for a few minutes, then shape into flat burgers.

Heat a heavy-based non-stick pan with the oil brushed over it and fry the burgers over medium to high heat for 6 minutes on each side.

BOMBAY SUPPER

This one-dish equivalent to curry-and-rice is a bit like an Indian risotto. Try it with a yogurt and cucumber relish.

Calories per serving: 385
Saturated fat: Medium
Total fat: Low
Protein: Medium
Carbohydrate: High
Cholesterol: Nil
Vitamins: A, C, E
Minerals: Potassium, Iron, Zinc

1 tbsp olive oil
15 g / ½ oz low-fat spread
1 large onion, finely chopped
2 peppers (1 green, 1 yellow), deseeded and chopped
325 g / 12 oz parboiled potatoes
1 heaped tbsp *Curry Powder* (see page 122)
1½ tsp garam masala
1½ tsp ground cumin
1 large or 2 medium aubergines
825 ml / 1½ pints *Vegetable Stock* (see page 122)
175 g / 6 oz Basmati rice, rinsed
one 400 g / 14 oz can of tomatoes
juice of ½ lemon
1 level tbsp brown sugar
15 g / ½ oz creamed coconut
2 heaped tbsp tomato purée
salt

Heat the oil and low-fat spread in a large frying pan and sauté the onion and peppers until soft.

Cut the potatoes into bite-sized pieces. Add these with the spices to the pan and stir for 2 minutes. Top and tail the aubergines and cut into bite-sized pieces, then add these. Add the stock to the pan and bring to the boil. Turn the heat down and add all the other ingredients.

Simmer until the rice and vegetables are tender. Taste and adjust the seasoning if necessary.

Note: new potatoes are best for this dish, although any old waxy variety can be used.

POLENTA AND PEPPERS

Polenta is also nice cooked in the same way as here, but using the Mediterranean Sauce on page 67 rather than the pepper mix.

Calories per serving: 205
Saturated fat: High
Total fat: High
Protein: Medium
Carbohydrate: Low
Cholesterol: 6.5 mg
Vitamins: A, B group, D
Minerals: Potassium, Iron,
*   Calcium*

75 g / 3 oz polenta cornmeal
1 dsp chopped basil
40 g / 1½ reduced-fat Cheddar, grated
15 g / ½ oz reduced-fat cooking
    spread
2 tbsp olive oil
325 g / 12 oz mixed peppers,
    deseeded and sliced
1 small garlic clove, chopped
3 tbsp dry white wine
50 g / 2 oz fresh leaf spinach
1 dsp balsamic vinegar
1 tsp fresh thyme
salt and black pepper

Make the polenta well ahead. Bring 425 ml / 15 fl oz lightly salted water to the boil and sprinkle in the polenta. Reduce the heat and cook for 20 minutes, stirring from time to time, or until the polenta comes away from the sides of the pan.

Stir in the basil, cheese and cooking spread, then transfer the mixture to a tin brushed with ½ tablespoon of olive oil. Leave to cool and harden.

When the polenta is quite solid, heat 1 tablespoon of olive oil in a frying pan and stir-fry the peppers and garlic for 15 minutes until soft.

Add the wine and bring to a bubble. Add the spinach, vinegar, thyme and seasonings and remove from the heat.

Meanwhile, cut the cooled solidified polenta into about 32 pieces. Brush these with the remaining olive oil and grill for 5 minutes. Turn them over and grill again until golden. Serve the polenta with the peppers.

HOT CHEESE AND OLIVE PLATTER

This is the quickest supper you could organize. It's a bit higher in fat than is perfect, but it has much less saturated fat and total fat than a typical 'Cheddar and biscuits' supper.

Calories per serving: 350
Saturated fat: High
Total fat: High
Protein: High
Carbohydrate: Low
Cholesterol: 50 mg
Vitamins: A, B group, E
Minerals: Calcium, Iron

1 tbsp olive oil
225 g / 8 oz Haloumi cheese, cubed
8 stoned black olives
2 sun-dried tomatoes in oil, drained
    and chopped
juice of ½ lemon, to serve
225 g / 8 oz French bread, cut into
    4 chunks, to serve

Heat the olive oil in a frying pan over a low to medium heat and fry the cheese, olives and sun-dried tomatoes, turning occasionally for a few minutes.

Serve with lemon juice and hot French bread.

OPPOSITE: Polenta and Peppers; Hot Cheese and Olive Platter

THREE-BEAN CASSEROLE

You can vary the types of beans used according to what you have in the cupboard.

Calories per serving: 290
Saturated fat: Low
Total fat: Low
Protein: Low
Carbohydrate: High
Cholesterol: Nil
Vitamins: B group, A, C, E
Minerals: Calcium, Potassium,
   Iron, Zinc, Magnesium

1 tbsp olive oil
1 large onion, thinly sliced
2 garlic cloves, crushed
two 400 g / 14 oz cans of chopped
   tomatoes (with liquid)
2 tbsp tomato purée
125 ml / 4½ fl oz dry white wine
1 tbsp red wine vinegar
1 dsp runny honey
250 g / 9 oz (drained weight) each
   canned borlotti, cannellini and
   adzuki beans
about 250 ml / ½ pint *Vegetable Stock*
   (see page 122)
salt and black pepper

Heat the oil in a flameproof casserole or large frying pan which has a lid and sauté the onion and garlic until soft.

Add the tomatoes, tomato purée and wine. Bring to the boil and boil gently for 2 minutes.

Stir in the vinegar and honey. Then mix in the beans and seasoning and simmer very gently for 30 minutes, topping up with vegetable stock as necessary to give a rich sauce (the dish shouldn't get too dry).

MACARONI, RED PEPPER AND BROCCOLI BAKE

To reduce the fat in this dish even further you could use reduced-fat cooking spread instead of butter in the sauce. However, the fat content here is actually only 21% in total anyway.

Calories per serving: 415
Saturated fat: High
Total fat: Medium
Protein: High
Carbohydrate: High
Cholesterol: 25 mg
Vitamins: A, C, E, B group, D
Minerals: Calcium, Iron,
   Magnesium, Potassium

225 g / 8 oz (dry weight) macaroni
225 g / 8 oz broccoli florets
225 g / 8 oz red peppers, deseeded,
   sliced and cut into 2 cm / ¾ in
   lengths
25 g / 1 oz butter
25 g / 1 oz plain flour
500 ml / 18 fl oz skimmed milk
100 g / 3½ oz reduced-fat Cheddar
   cheese, grated
salt and black pepper

Preheat the oven to 200°C / 400°F / gas6 and grease the baking dish lightly with a little of the butter.

Cook the macaroni in a large pan of boiling salted water until it is tender but still firm to the bite. Drain immediately.

Blanch the broccoli and red pepper in boiling salted water for 3 minutes, drain immediately and arrange the vegetables and pasta in the baking dish.

Melt the butter in a saucepan and add the flour. Stir and cook over medium heat for 2 minutes. Add the milk and stir until the sauce thickens. Add seasoning and three-quarters of the cheese and stir again.

Thin the sauce down to a pouring consistency with a little water, then pour it over the bake and top with the remaining cheese.

Bake for about 20 minutes, until the top is brown.

SUMMER FRITTATA

*Serve this low-calorie –
but high-fat – dish with
plenty of crusty bread and
green salad.*

Calories per serving: 200
Saturated fat: High
Total fat: High
Protein: High
Carbohydrate: Low
Cholesterol: 375 mg
Vitamins: A, B group, C, D, E
Minerals: Iron, Potassium,
  Calcium

1 tbsp corn oil
4 medium courgettes, sliced
1 small red pepper, deseeded and
  thinly sliced
1 garlic clove, chopped
6 medium eggs, lightly beaten
4 tbsp sun-dried tomatoes in oil,
  drained well and chopped
6 spring onions, trimmed and chopped
1 tbsp fresh basil
1 tbsp fresh mint
25 g / 1 oz reduced-fat Cheddar
  cheese, grated
salt and black pepper

Heat the oil in a large non-stick frying pan and cook the courgettes and red pepper for 10 minutes, or until they are fairly soft. Add the garlic and stir for a minute.

Put the eggs, tomatoes, spring onions, herbs and seasoning in a bowl and combine well. Preheat the grill to hot.

Reduce the heat under the pan and pour in the egg mixture. Allow it to run under the vegetables. Cook over a low heat until the base of the frittata is golden.

Sprinkle the cheese over the top and place the pan under the grill until the top is golden.

Serve hot or cold, cut into wedges.

BAKMIE GORENG

*This is supposed to be
quite a dry stir-fry but you
can add a little vegetable
stock towards the end of
cooking.*

Calories per serving: 325
Saturated fat: Low
Total fat: Medium
Protein: Medium
Carbohydrate: High
Cholesterol: 55 mg
Vitamins: A, B group, C, E
Minerals: Potassium

225 g / 8 oz egg-thread noodles
2 tbsp sunflower oil
5 shallots, thinly sliced
225 g / 8 oz mixed mushrooms
2 garlic cloves, crushed
2 medium carrots, diced
50 g / 2 oz (4 large) Chinese leaves
100 g / 3½ oz mixed beansprouts
2 tomatoes, skinned, deseeded and
  chopped
4 spring onions, chopped
2 tbsp soy sauce
salt and black pepper
chopped parsley to garnish

Soak the noodles according to the packet instructions.

While the noodles are soaking, heat the oil in a wok or large non-stick frying pan over a moderate heat and stir-fry the shallots for 2 minutes. Add the mushrooms, garlic and carrots and fry for 2 minutes more. Add the Chinese leaves and stir-fry for 1 minute.

Drain the noodles and add them to the pan together with the beansprouts, tomatoes, spring onions, soy sauce and black pepper. Fry until the noodles are nice and hot.

Taste and adjust the seasoning if necessary. Serve immediately, garnished with parsley.

CHANA MASALEDAR

*With pitta or other flat
bread, this makes a good
quick supper.*

Calories per serving: 157
Saturated fat: Medium
Total fat: Medium
Protein: High
Carbohydrate: High
Cholesterol: Nil
Vitamins: B group, E
Minerals: Calcium, Iron,
  Magnesium, Potassium

1¼ tbsp corn or sunflower oil
½ tsp whole cumin seeds
1 medium onion, chopped
1 tsp ground coriander
2 level tsp garam masala
knob of fresh ginger, finely chopped
pinch of cayenne pepper
1 large garlic clove, crushed
1 tbsp tomato purée
350 g / 12 oz (drained weight, but
  reserving liquid) canned chickpeas
1 tbsp lemon juice
salt

Heat the oil in a frying pan and add the cumin seeds and onion. Sauté until the onion is soft and barely golden. Reduce the heat and add the rest of the spices and the garlic. Stir for a minute or two.

Add the tomato purée, chickpeas and 150 ml / 5½ fl oz of the reserved chickpea liquid and the lemon juice. Stir to blend well, cover and simmer for 30 minutes.

Taste and adjust the seasoning with a little salt if necessary.

THAI-STYLE MIXED VEGETABLES WITH CHILLI

You can make this dish as hot or as mild as you like – either way it is tasty and easy to make. I serve it with rice for a filling low-calorie supper.

Calories per serving: 150
Saturated fat: High
Total fat: High
Protein: Medium
Carbohydrate: Low
Cholesterol: Nil
Vitamins: C, E, Folic acid
Minerals: Potassium

2 tbsp corn oil
1 tbsp coriander seeds, ground
small knob of fresh ginger, peeled and chopped
5 red chillies, deseeded and finely chopped, *or* 2 dsp Sambal Oelek paste
200 g / 7 oz whole green beans, cut in half
100 g / 3½ oz baby sweetcorn
200 g / 7 oz small cauliflower florets
1 dsp ground turmeric
200 g / 7 oz whole button mushrooms
little *Vegetable Stock* (see page 122)
200 ml / 7 fl oz thick coconut milk
1 tsp lemon grass, soaked in water for 15 minutes if not using fresh
lime wedges and lime juice
1 dsp chopped fresh coriander leaves
salt

Heat the oil in a wok or heavy-based frying pan and add the ground coriander seeds, ginger and chillies or paste. Stir for 2 minutes, then add the beans, sweetcorn, cauliflower, turmeric and a little salt. Stir-fry the vegetables for 2 minutes.

Add the whole mushrooms and stir-fry for 1 minute. Add a little vegetable stock to prevent sticking, if necessary.

Add the coconut milk and lemon grass and a dash of lime juice. Simmer for a minute and serve garnished with fresh coriander and lime wedges.

CHINESE EGG AND NOODLE STIR-FRY

This dish is totally delicious, quick to cook and works just as well if the quantities are reduced to make a one-person supper.

Calories per serving: 420
Saturated fat: Medium
Total fat: Medium
Protein: High
Carbohydrate: Medium
Cholesterol: 300 mg
Vitamins: A, B group, D, E, C
Minerals: Iron, Potassium

225 g / 8 oz egg-thread noodles
1 tbsp sunflower oil
4 spring onions, chopped
1 garlic clove, crushed
knob of root ginger, peeled and finely chopped
50 g / 2 oz bamboo shoots
25 g / 1 oz water chestnuts, sliced
50 g / 2 oz cashew nuts
50 g / 2 oz button mushrooms
1 tbsp dry sherry
100 g / 3½ oz fresh beansprouts
4 medium eggs, lightly beaten
salt

Soak the noodles according to the packet instructions while you cook the stir-fry.

Heat the oil in a wok or non-stick frying pan and stir-fry the spring onions, garlic and ginger for a minute.

Add the bamboo shoots, water chestnuts, cashew nuts, mushrooms and sherry and stir for a minute. Add the beansprouts, eggs and salt and cook, stirring, until the eggs are scrambled.

Drain the noodles and serve the stir-fry on them.

DELHI-STYLE CAULIFLOWER

This tasty curry makes a complete meal if you serve it with a lentil or chickpea dhal (see Chana Masaledar *page 77) and some brown or Basmati rice.*

Calories per serving: 155
Saturated fat: Low
Total fat: High
Protein: Medium
Carbohydrate: Medium
Cholesterol: Trace
Vitamins: C
Minerals: Iron

1 tbsp corn or sunflower oil
1 small onion, finely chopped
1 tbsp *Curry Powder* (see page 122)
1 garlic clove
450 g / 1 lb cauliflower florets
50 g / 2 oz green beans, trimmed and cut into two
1 tbsp plain wholemeal flour
400 ml / 14 fl oz *Vegetable Stock* (see page 122)
40 g / 1½ oz sultanas
25 g / 1 oz flaked almonds
100 ml / 3½ fl oz natural low-fat yogurt
2.5 cm / 1 in piece of cucumber, chopped, to garnish
fresh coriander leaves, to garnish

Heat the oil in a frying pan and add the onion. Stir-fry it for a few minutes until soft. Add the curry powder and garlic and stir for 2 minutes.

Add the cauliflower and beans. Stir and cook, covered, for a few minutes.

Stir in the flour thoroughly, followed by the stock and sultanas. Bring to a simmer, stirring gently, and let simmer, covered, for 12 minutes or until the cauliflower is just tender – don't overcook.

Add the almonds at the last minute. Just before serving, dribble the yogurt over the dish and garnish with cucumber and coriander.

TAGLIATELLE WITH WINE AND MUSHROOMS

You can use whatever mushrooms you like or can buy, but this dish is improved by having at least two different kinds – although don't use Chinese dried mushrooms.

Calories per serving: 355
Saturated fat: Medium
Total fat: Medium
Protein: Medium
Carbohydrate: High
Cholesterol: 20 mg
Vitamins: A, C, Folic acid, Niacin, E
Minerals: Iron, Potassium

225 g / 8 oz tagliatelle or other flat ribbon pasta
1½ tbsp olive oil
1 medium onion, chopped
2 garlic cloves, crushed
450 g / 1 lb mixed mushrooms (eg button, yellow oysters, brown oysters, shiitake, brown caps), chopped or torn
15 g / ½ oz butter
1 tbsp plain flour
about 200 ml / 7 fl oz *Vegetable Stock* (see page 122)
50 ml / 2 fl oz dry white wine
2 tbsp chopped basil
3 tbsp extra-thick single cream
salt and black pepper
chopped chives or parsley, to garnish
1 tbsp grated Parmesan cheese, to garnish

Put the pasta in plenty of lightly salted boiling water together with ½ tablespoon of the oil and boil for 10 minutes for dried pasta or 3–5 minutes for fresh.

Heat the remaining oil in a heavy non-stick pan and sauté the onion and garlic until soft and just turning golden. Add the mushrooms and stir. Remove from the heat, but keep the contents of the pan warm.

Melt the butter in a small saucepan, add the flour and cook for 1 minute. Add the stock and wine and bring to a bubble. Add the basil and stir until you have a sauce.

Add this sauce to the frying pan and return it to the heat. Add the cream and heat through.

Drain the pasta when it is tender but still firm to the bite. Serve it with sauce poured over and garnished with chives and Parmesan.

TOFU AND VEGETABLE MEDLEY

I find the delicate texture of silken firm tofu nicer in this dish, but you can use ordinary tofu if you like. Serve with a grain of your choice – brown rice and couscous are nice.

Calories per serving: 172
Saturated fat: Low
Total fat: High
Protein: High
Carbohydrate: Low
Cholesterol: Nil
Vitamins: A, C
Minerals: Calcium, Potassium, Iron

1 tbsp sunflower oil
1 onion, thinly sliced
2 garlic cloves, crushed
2 carrots, cut into julienne strips
2 celery stalks, cut into julienne strips
50 g / 2 oz green beans, halved
50 g / 2 oz water chestnuts, sliced
50 g / 2 oz mushrooms, sliced
one 400 g / 14 oz can tomatoes
250 ml / ½ pint *Vegetable Stock* (see page 122)
4 tbsp light soy sauce
1 tbsp cider vinegar
1 tbsp honey
1 tbsp tomato purée
1 tbsp cornflour
325 g / 12 oz silken firm tofu, cut into strips
100 g / 3½ oz fresh beansprouts

Heat the oil in a flameproof casserole dish or in a heavy-bottomed frying pan which has a lid and fry the onion, garlic, carrots, celery, beans and water chestnuts for 3 minutes.

Add the mushrooms, tomatoes, stock, soy sauce, vinegar, honey and tomato purée, stirring well. Bring to boil, reduce the heat, cover and simmer for 15 minutes.

Mix the cornflour with 1 tablespoon of water and add to the pan. Stir thoroughly.

Add the strips of tofu and the beansprouts. Stir again gently and serve.

FALAFEL PATTIES

I find the canned sweet pepper gives a lovely moist texture to these patties, but you can use a very finely chopped fresh pepper. The patties go marvellously well with pitta bread, salad and Fresh Tomato Salsa *or* Light Mayonnaise *(see pages 67 and 124).*

Calories per serving: 156
Saturated fat: Medium
Total fat: Medium
Protein: Medium
Carbohydrate: Medium
Cholesterol: 68 mg
Vitamins: C, E
Minerals: Iron

275 g / 10 oz chickpeas (soaked weight), soaked and cooked as described on page 18 or one 425 g / 15 oz can, drained
1 small onion, very finely chopped
1 canned sweet red pepper, drained and finely chopped
1 garlic clove, crushed
1 tbsp chopped parsley
1 tsp ground cumin
1 tsp ground coriander
pinch of ground chilli
1 egg, beaten
1 tbsp corn oil
salt and black pepper
little wholemeal flour for coating

Mash the chickpeas with a fork or whizz them in a blender to make a coarse purée.

In a bowl, mix the chickpea purée with the onion, pepper, garlic, parsley, spices, seasoning and egg. Using your hands, form the mixture into 12 small egg- or sausage-shaped patties.

Heat the oil in a non-stick frying pan and coat each patty lightly in flour before frying over a medium heat for about 10 minutes until golden, turning at least once.

Main courses

If you have a little time to spare or feel like trying something new, these main-course recipes will please both family and friends.

My test of a good vegetarian recipe is whether my carnivorous friends find it enjoyable too. All the recipes in this chapter have been declared successes by all kinds of people: from children to teenagers; from meat-eaters to committed vegetarians.

Few need a great deal of cooking skills, but all have the merit of winning you a reputation as a good 'tasty' cook. Not one would be regarded by the anti-health food brigade as too worthy, yet all can be included in any maintenance or slimming diet without guilt. I've reduced the fat content of each to that which is truly necessary, and virtually all provide an abundance of fibre, vitamins, minerals and protein.

For other main-course ideas, read the Vegetarian Kitchen chapter (page 16) and there are also cold main courses in the next chapter and suppers in the previous chapter that can be 'dressed up' a little with the addition of side salads.

Once you have tried these recipes you can confidently experiment with variations of your own. For instance, try baking pancakes filled with the Crispy Vegetable Pie filling (page 86), stuff baked vegetables with your own mix of grains, seeds and vegetables, or mix all kinds of pulses with all kinds of vegetables in casseroles.

Even pastry can form part of a healthy diet. Try the wholemeal shortcrust flan filled with various vegetables, egg and some reduced-fat cheese – or use lower-calorie filo pastry as a crispy base for a sauté of Mediterranean vegetables.

Rice and grains are an ideal starting point for many a main-course pilaff or risotto – various nuts, seeds, vegetables, stock and flavourings can give you dozens of different styles of meal with only your imagination to limit you!

Grilled Vegetables with Bulghar (page 84)

GRILLED VEGETABLES WITH BULGHAR

Sometimes the simplest things taste the most delicious – and this is one.

Calories per serving: 340
Saturated fat: Low
Total fat: Medium
Protein: Medium
Carbohydrate: High
Cholesterol: Nil
Vitamins: C, A, B group, E
Minerals: Iron, Potassium, Magnesium

225 g / 8 oz bulghar wheat
550 ml / 1 pint hot *Vegetable Stock* (see page 122)
1 large garlic clove, crushed
2 tbsp olive oil
200 g / 7 oz large brown-cap mushrooms, halved
2 medium aubergines, sliced lengthwise
200 g / 7 oz mixed peppers, deseeded and chopped into squares
2 small courgettes, sliced lengthwise
8 canned artichoke hearts (one 400 g / 14 oz can) drained and halved
8 sun-dried tomatoes in oil, drained, patted dry and chopped
2 tbsp balsamic vinegar
1 tbsp freshly chopped basil

Soak the bulghar in the hot vegetable stock for 30 minutes. Towards the end of that time, preheat the oven to 180°C / 350°F / gas4.

Drain off any excess liquid from the bulghar and transfer to an ovenproof dish that has a lid. Cover and put in the oven while you prepare the vegetables. Preheat the grill to medium.

Place the garlic in a bowl with the oil and mix well together. Brush the vegetables with the oil mixture and put them all except the artichokes on the grill pan.

Grill for 5 minutes, turning once. Add the artichokes for the last minute to warm them.

Serve the vegetables immediately over the warmed bulghar, with the sun-dried tomatoes, vinegar, basil, any pan juices and any remaining olive oil sprinkled over.

AUBERGINE AND LENTIL LAYER

This is one of my best ever slimmers' main meals – it is so rich and filling you just wouldn't believe how low in calories and fat it is!

Calories per serving: 285
Saturated fat: Medium
Total fat: Medium
Protein: High
Carbohydrate: High
Cholesterol: 6 mg
Vitamins: A, B group, C, E
Minerals: Potassium, Iron, Zinc

1 large or 2 medium aubergines, topped and tailed
1 tbsp olive oil
1 medium onion, very thinly sliced
1 medium yellow pepper, deseeded and thinly sliced
1 garlic clove, crushed
450 g / 1 lb (cooked weight) brown lentils, pre-cooked (see pages 22–3)
1 tsp herbes de Provence
50 g / 2 oz well-drained sun-dried tomatoes in oil, chopped
325 ml / 12 fl oz passata
1 tbsp grated Parmesan cheese
50 g / 2 oz reduced-fat Cheddar cheese, grated
6 tbsp wholemeal breadcrumbs
salt and black pepper

Preheat the oven to 180°C / 350°F / gas4.

Slice the aubergines into rounds and blanch them for 3 minutes in boiling salted water. Drain on paper towels.

Heat the oil in a non-stick pan and stir-fry the onion and pepper over medium heat for about 15 minutes, until soft. Add the garlic and stir for 1 minute.

Layer half the lentils in a suitable baking dish, top with half the aubergine slices and half each of the onion mixture, herbs, sun-dried tomatoes, passata and some seasoning. Repeat the layers.

Mix together the cheeses and breadcrumbs, sprinkle this over the top and bake for 45 minutes.

Note: for extra flavour you can also bake, dry-fry or grill the aubergine slices instead of initially blanching them.

RICH POTATO BAKE

The topping for this dish can be used on any combination of vegetables in a bake in place of an ordinary cheese sauce.

Calories per serving: 438
Saturated fat: High
Total fat: Medium
Protein: High
Carbohydrate: High
Cholesterol: 19 mg
Vitamins: C, A, D, Folic acid
Minerals: Potassium, Calcium,
*   Iron*

1 tbsp olive oil
2 red onions, thinly sliced
700 g / 1 lb 10 oz waxy potatoes,
    scrubbed and sliced
2 garlic cloves, finely chopped
1 red and 1 yellow pepper, deseeded
    and chopped
2 medium courgettes, sliced
1 quantity *Tomato Sauce* (see page 69)
250 ml / ½ pint *Vegetable Stock*
    (see page 122)
1 tsp basil
225 g / 8 oz thick low-fat natural
    yogurt
1 tsp cornflour
100 g / 3½ oz Mozzarella cheese,
    grated
50 g / 2 oz reduced-fat Cheddar
    cheese, grated
50 g / 2 oz wholemeal breadcrumbs
salt and black pepper

Heat the oil in a large heavy-based frying pan and stir the onions over medium heat until soft. Add the potatoes, garlic, peppers and courgettes and stir for 5 minutes.

Add the tomato sauce and stock. Simmer, covered, for 1 hour or until the potatoes are tender. Taste and adjust the seasoning. Add the basil and a little extra stock if necessary.

Preheat the oven to 200°C / 400°F / gas6 or the grill to medium.

Transfer the mixture to 4 gratin dishes or 1 shallow baking dish. Beat together the yogurt and cornflour and mix in half the cheeses. Spread across the centre of the dish or dishes. Top with the remaining cheeses and breadcrumbs mixed together. Brown in the oven or under the grill for 5–10 minutes.
Note: if you are in a hurry and don't have any home-made tomato sauce to hand, you could use a jar of passata and add extra basil and seasoning.

HEREFORD HOT-POT

This tasty winter casserole is a complete meal in itself. If you're very hungry, however, you could serve it in large bowls like a soup, accompanied by crusty bread to mop up the lovely cidery juices.

Calories per serving: 375
Saturated fat: Medium
Total fat: Low
Protein: High
Carbohydrate: High
Cholesterol: 7 mg
Vitamins: A, B group, C, D
Minerals: Calcium, Potassium,
*   Iron, Magnesium, Zinc*

1 dsp sunflower oil
3 medium leeks, washed and sliced
1 large onion, sliced
325 g / 12 oz swede, cubed
225 g / 8 oz carrots, sliced
25 g / 1 oz plain flour
550 ml / 1 pint dry cider
1 tbsp tomato purée
1 tbsp yeast extract
1 small dessert apple, cored and sliced
175 g / 6 oz pre-cooked red lentils
450 g / 1 lb potatoes, parboiled for
    3 minutes and sliced
1 good tsp butter
75 g / 3 oz reduced-fat Cheddar
    cheese, grated
salt and black pepper

Preheat the oven to 180°C / 350°F / gas4.

Heat the oil in a heavy-based flameproof casserole and sweat the leeks, onions, swede and carrots over a low heat, covered with a lid, for about 15 minutes until softened a little.

Meanwhile, in a small saucepan, mix the flour to a paste with a little of the cider over a medium heat. Gradually add the rest of the cider, stirring. Mix in the tomato purée, yeast extract, salt and pepper.

Chop the apple and add it to the vegetables in the casserole together with the lentils, then pour the cider sauce over. Arrange the potato slices on top, put tiny dots of the butter over them and scatter the cheese over the top.

Cover and bake for 1½ hours. Uncover for the last 30 minutes of cooking time to allow the topping to brown.
Note: depending on variety of potato and age of vegetables, cooking time may need to be extended. If it looks like getting too dry when you remove the lid for the last half hour, carefully add a little water in between the layer of potato and the side of the pan.

CRISPY VEGETABLE PIE

This delicately flavoured and pretty pie is easy to make, but does take a while to assemble. It is ideal both for family meals and entertaining. You will add even more flavour to this dish if you have time to preheat the skimmed milk slowly, infusing in it a bay leaf, a chopped carrot and some black peppercorns.

Calories per serving: 600 for 4; 400 for 6
Saturated fat: Medium
Total fat: Medium
Protein: Medium
Carbohydrate: Medium
Cholesterol: 24 mg
Vitamins: A, C, E
Minerals: Calcium, Potassium

1 large leek, sliced
4 carrots, cubed
1 parsnip, cubed
2 courgettes, cubed
1 small (about 115 g / 4 oz) head of broccoli
75 g / 3 oz yellow split peas, cooked (see chart on page 23)
40 g / 1½ oz butter
1½ tbsp plain flour
200 ml / 7 fl oz skimmed milk
1 tbsp olive oil
6 oblong sheets of filo pastry (about 115 g / 4 oz)
salt and black pepper

Preheat the oven to 190°C / 375°F / gas5.

Boil the leek, carrots and parsnip in a saucepan of lightly salted water until barely cooked. Drain, reserving the cooking water.

In a separate pan, boil the courgettes and broccoli for 2 minutes. Drain, then divide the broccoli into small florets.

Arrange the vegetables and split peas in a 27 x 22 cm / 11 x 8½ in ovenproof dish.

Melt 25 g / 1 oz of the butter in a saucepan and add the flour, stirring for a minute or two until you have a thick roux. Gradually add the milk (see left), stirring, until you have a thick sauce. Add 850 ml / 1½ pints of the reserved vegetable water and stir. Adjust the seasoning. Pour the sauce evenly over the vegetables.

Melt the remaining butter with the olive oil in a small pan. Making sure that the butter isn't hot, brush each of the first 4 sheets of filo pastry and place carefully over the vegetables.

Brush the last 2 sheets with the remaining oil and butter mixture and use each to cover half of the top, gathering each into loose folds (rather like drawn curtains). This both looks attractive and gives a much greater 'crispy' area when the pie comes out of the oven.

Bake for about 25 minutes, or until the top is deep golden brown and crisp.

CHEESE AND TOMATO ROULADE

Roulades are surprisingly easy to prepare and make perfect light summer dishes if you are slimming. They can also be used as starters for dinner parties.

Calories per serving: 225
Saturated fat: High
Total fat: High
Protein: High
Carbohydrate: Low
Cholesterol: 260 mg
Vitamins: A, B group, D, E, C
Minerals: Calcium, Iron, Potassium

15 g / ½ oz reduced-fat cooking spread
25 g / 1 oz plain flour
450 g / 1 lb fresh ripe tomatoes, blanched, skinned and finely chopped
4 eggs, separated
for the filling:
225 g / 8 oz low-fat soft cheese
4 tbsp 0%-fat fromage frais
4 spring onions, finely chopped
2 tsp each chopped parsley and thyme
salt and black pepper

Preheat the oven to 190°C / 375°F / gas5. Line a roulade (Swiss roll) tin with non-stick baking paper.

Melt the spread in a saucepan. Add the flour and simmer for 1 minute. Stir in the tomatoes and continue to stir for 5 minutes. Remove from heat, season and stir in the egg yolks.

Whisk the egg whites to stiff peaks and fold into the tomato mixture. Spoon into the tin and bake for 15–20 minutes, until firm.

Meanwhile, prepare the filling: in a bowl, mix the soft cheese and fromage frais. Add the spring onions, herbs and some seasoning.

Turn the roulade out. Spread the filling over it and roll it up, removing the baking paper as you go. Serve warm.

OPPOSITE: Crispy Vegetable Pie; Cheese and Tomato Roulade

SPICY STUFFED VEGETABLES

You can use a variety of vegetables for this dish – for a nice change use the mixture to stuff as many varieties of baby vegetables as you can get!

Calories per serving: about 400
  (depending on the vegetables
  used)
Saturated fat: Low
Total fat: Low
Protein: Medium
Carbohydrate: High
Cholesterol: Nil
Vitamins: C, A, E
Minerals: Iron, Potassium, Zinc

4 large green peppers, halved
  lengthwise and deseeded, or
  vegetables of choice suitable for
  stuffing to serve 4, eg 2 large
  aubergines, 4 large courgettes or
  small squash, or 4 beef tomatoes
for the stuffing:
1 tbsp corn oil
225 g / 8 oz Basmati rice, washed and
  drained
2 tsp *Curry Powder* (see page 122)
about 550 ml / 1 pint *Vegetable Stock*
  (see page 122)
1 celery stalk, chopped small
50 g / 2 oz sultanas
1 small red eating apple
knob of brown sugar
1 dsp lemon juice
1 small red pepper, deseeded and
  chopped small
25 g / 1 oz cashew or mixed nuts,
  chopped
1 tbsp chopped parsley

Preheat the oven to 180°C / 350°F / gas4.

Heat the oil in a large non-stick frying pan over a moderate heat. Stir in the rice and curry powder and stir for a minute. Pour in the stock and the rest of the stuffing ingredients. Bring to a simmer, lower the heat and simmer for 20 minutes, adding further stock or water if necessary.

Meanwhile, blanch the peppers in boiling salted water for 2 minutes, drain immediately and pat dry. If using aubergines, scoop out half the flesh and either use it for a purée or mix with stuffing ingredients. Prepare courgettes or squash in the same way, but the spare flesh is best discarded. Beef tomatoes should be prepared by removing a slice off the top, and scooping out the seedy flesh. The tomatoes don't need blanching.

Fill the pepper halves or other vegetables with the stuffing and arrange in a baking dish with a little stock in its base. Cover with foil and bake for 30 minutes, or until the vegetables are tender.

COBBLER-TOPPED CASSEROLE

This cobbler (scone) topping is a good alternative to pastry as it is delicious but much lower in fat and calories.

Calories per serving: 380
Saturated fat: High
Total fat: Medium
Protein: High
Carbohydrate: High
Cholesterol: 21 mg
Vitamins: B group, C, A
Minerals: Calcium, Iron,
  Magnesium, Potassium

200 g / 7 oz courgettes, sliced
50 g / 2 oz mushrooms, sliced
2 leeks, trimmed and sliced
225 g / 8 oz (drained weight) canned
  or pre-cooked butter beans
100 g / 3½ oz (drained weight) canned
  or pre-cooked red kidney beans
100 g / 3½ oz (drained weight) canned
  or pre-cooked black-eye beans
350 ml / 12½ fl oz *Vegetable Stock*
  (see page 122)
2 tbsp tomato purée
dash of vegetarian Worcestershire
  sauce
salt and black pepper
for the scone topping:
175 g / 6 oz self-raising flour
2 level tsp baking powder
1 heaped tsp herbes de Provence
40 g / 1½ oz butter or vegetarian
  margarine
4 good tbsp natural yogurt

Preheat the oven to 200°C / 400°F / gas6.

Arrange all the vegetables and beans in flameproof casserole. Mix the stock, tomato purée, Worcestershire sauce and seasoning and pour over the vegetables and beans. Simmer or bake for 30 minutes.

Meanwhile, make the topping: sift the flour into a mixing bowl with the baking powder, herbs and a pinch of salt. Rub in the butter or margarine. Stir in the yogurt and mix. Knead lightly on a floured board.

Roll out to a thickness of about 1 cm / ½ in and cut out 4 cm / 1½ in rounds with a pastry cutter. Arrange these on top of the casserole and bake for 30 minutes, until the scone topping is golden.

BROCCOLI AND SWEETCORN FLAN

Calories per serving: 300
Saturated fat: High
Total fat: High
Protein: High
Carbohydrate: Low
Cholesterol: 187 mg
Vitamins: A, B group, D, C, E
Minerals: Iron, Calcium,
  Potassium

1 quantity *Wholemeal Shortcrust Pastry* (see page 120)
200 g / 7 oz broccoli florets
100 g / 3½ oz sweetcorn kernels
1 dsp olive oil
1 small onion, finely chopped
3 tbsp chopped fresh parsley
3 medium eggs, beaten
175 g / 6 oz 0%-fat fromage frais
salt and black pepper

Preheat the oven to 190°C / 375°F / gas5.
Line a 20 cm / 8 in flan tin with the pastry and bake blind for 10 minutes.
Meanwhile, parboil the broccoli florets and sweetcorn in lightly salted water until barely cooked (about 4 minutes). Drain immediately.
Heat the oil in a small frying pan over a moderate heat and cook the onion until soft. Stir in the drained vegetables, parsley and some seasoning.
Combine the eggs and fromage frais in a bowl. Arrange the vegetables over the flan base and pour over the egg mixture.
Bake for 30 minutes, or until the filling is set and golden.

CASHEW ROAST

With a little extra stock this makes a good filling for stuffed vegetables; or turn it into a vegetable cottage pie by topping it with mashed potato.

Calories per serving: 390
Saturated fat: High
Total fat: High
Protein: Medium
Carbohydrate: Low
Cholesterol: Nil
Vitamins: B group, A, C
Minerals: Iron, Potassium

1 tbsp corn oil
1 medium onion, finely chopped
1 garlic clove, chopped
2 tsp yeast extract
300 ml / ½ pint *Vegetable Stock* (see page 122)
200 g / 7 oz cashew nuts, coarsely ground
110 g / 4 oz wholemeal breadcrumbs
1 medium carrot, grated
1 tsp mixed herbs
salt and black pepper

Preheat the oven to 190°C / 375°F / gas5.
Heat the oil in a non-stick frying pan over a moderate heat and sauté the onion and garlic until soft.
Mix the yeast extract into the stock and bring to the boil. Add all the remaining ingredients, season and combine well. Turn the mixture into a 900 g / 2 lb loaf tin and flatten the surface.
Bake for 45 minutes.

PROVENÇAL PANCAKES WITH CHEESE SAUCE

Calories per serving: 347
Saturated fat: Medium
Total fat: High
Protein: High
Carbohydrate: Medium
Cholesterol: 69 mg
Vitamins: A, B group, C, D, E
Minerals; Calcium, Iron,
  Potassium

1 batch *Mediterranean Sauce* (see page 67)
1 quantity *Cheese Sauce* (see page 67)
1 batch *Pancakes* (see page 121)
2 tbsp chopped fresh parsley

Make up all the components, cooking the pancakes last. Preheat the oven to 200°C / 400°F / gas6.
Spoon one-eighth of the sauce mixture on one side of each pancake and roll it up. Then carefully place in an oblong baking dish. Carry on until all are filled this way.
Pour the cheese sauce evenly over the pancakes and bake until the sauce is bubbling. Garnish with the parsley to serve.

CHEESE AND ONION BREAD BAKE

This is a cheese-lover's delight and makes a really robust meal – it needs only a large mixed salad to go with it.

Calories per serving: 450
Saturated fat: High
Total fat: High
Protein: High
Carbohydrate: Medium
Cholesterol: 210 mg
Vitamins: A, B group, C, D, E
Minerals: Calcium, Iron,
    Magnesium, Potassium

1 tbsp corn oil
1 large onion, finely chopped
½ tsp thyme
125 g / 4½ oz reduced-fat Cheddar
    cheese, grated
75 g / 3 oz Parmesan cheese, grated
1 dsp freshly chopped chives
8 medium slices of wholemeal bread,
    crusts removed
3 medium eggs
500 ml / 18 fl oz skimmed milk
black pepper

Preheat the oven to 190°C / 375°F / gas5 and brush an oblong baking dish with a little oil.

Heat the remaining oil in a frying pan and fry the onions with the thyme over a gentle heat, stirring occasionally, for 15–20 minutes until very soft and just turning golden. Mix the cheeses and the chives in a small bowl.

Put 4 slices of bread on the bottom of the prepared dish, ensuring that they fit exactly. Cover with the onion mixture and half the cheese mixture. Put the other slices of bread over and cover with the remaining cheese.

Whisk the eggs and milk together in a bowl and season with pepper. Pour this over the bread and cheese mixture. Bake for 30 minutes, or until puffed up and golden.

MEDITERRANEAN FILO TARTS

This is a very simple dish to make, but it is quite delicious. Use small tart tins and halve the quantities to make a delightful starter.

If using Haloumi cheese, which isn't as salty as Feta, you might like to add a little sea salt.

There are several variations you can try with this dish: for a lighter course, you could omit the avocado; Spanish canned piquillo peppers are a tasty and easy substitute for the home-grilled red peppers – allow 2 per person, and drain well.

Calories per serving: 325
Saturated fat: Medium
Total fat: Medium
Protein: Medium
Carbohydrate: Low
Cholesterol: 22 mg
Vitamins: A, C, D, E
Minerals: Calcium

4 red peppers. deseeded and
    quartered
8 sheets of filo pastry, cut into sixteen
    12.5 cm / 5 in squares (discard any
    surplus)
1 tbsp olive oil
100 g / 3½ oz Feta or Haloumi cheese,
    cut into small squares
4 juicy black olives, stoned and
    chopped
100 g / 3½ oz just-ripe avocado,
    peeled, stoned and chopped at the
    last minute
2 medium spring onions, sliced into
    thin rounds
1 tbsp olive oil
black pepper
4 basil leaves, chopped, to garnish
    (optional)

Preheat a hot grill. Place the peppers on a non-stick baking tray, skin side up, and grill until the skins are black.

Place the peppers in a plastic bag for 15 minutes, then peel off the skins and cut the flesh into diamond shapes.

Preheat the oven to 180°C / 350°F / gas4.

Line 4 individual metal flan dishes with the filo sheets, each one very lightly brushed with oil (it doesn't matter if the oil doesn't cover all of each sheet). Arrange 4 sheets in each dish so that you have an even eight-pointed star shape.

Place the lined dishes on a baking sheet and bake for about 6 minutes, until the pastry is a very light golden brown. Leaving the oven on, remove the cases and allow to cool for a minute, then remove from the tins.

While the cases are cooling, combine the remaining ingredients, except the basil if using, in a bowl and divide between the pastry cases, making sure several pieces of cheese are visible on the top of each filling. Twist a little black pepper on top of each and garnish with a little basil if you have it.

Warm in the oven for about 10 minutes until the cheese pieces are going golden at the edges, then serve immediately.

OPPOSITE: Delhi-style Cauliflower (page 80); Mediterranean Filo Tarts

MUSHROOM PILAFF

For a change, try replacing half the mushrooms with ceps or other wild mushrooms to make this tasty dish even tastier. You can buy them dried and reconstitute them by soaking them in water.

Calories per serving: 400
Saturated fat: Low
Total fat: Medium
Protein: Low
Carbohydrate: High
Cholesterol: Nil
Vitamins: B, E
Minerals: Potassium

2 tbsp corn or olive oil
1 onion, finely chopped
1 small red pepper, deseeded and
  finely chopped
275 g / 10 oz brown rice (ordinary or
  easy-cook)
110 g / 4 oz brown-cap or mixed
  mushrooms, chopped
550 ml / 1 pint *Vegetable Stock*
  (see page 122)
2 tbsp chopped fresh parsley
25 g / 1 oz sunflower seeds
25 g / 1 oz flaked almonds
salt and black pepper

Heat half the oil in a non-stick frying pan and sauté the onion over a moderate heat until soft and just turning golden. Add the rest of the oil and the pepper and stir for 2 minutes. Add the rice and stir again.

Add the mushrooms, stock, seasoning and half the parsley and bring to the boil. Lower the heat, cover the pan and simmer for 20 minutes if using quick-cook rice or up to 45 minutes if using ordinary, adding more stock from time to time if necessary.

About 5 minutes before the end of cooking time, stir in the seeds and nuts. When the rice is tender and virtually all the liquid is absorbed, serve the pilaff sprinkled with the remaining parsley.

TOFU KEBABS WITH PEANUT SAUCE

Although low in calories, this dish is reasonably high in fat; serve it with plenty of grain – eg fragrant Thai rice – to make the complete meal low in fat.

Calories per serving: 240
Saturated fat: Medium
Total fat: High
Protein: High
Carbohydrate: Low
Cholesterol: Trace
Vitamins: A, C, E
Minerals: Calcium, Potassium,
  Iron, Zinc

2 carrots
2 medium courgettes
350 g / 12 oz smoked tofu, cubed
3 small red onions
1 small garlic clove
1 tbsp olive oil
salt and black pepper
for the peanut sauce:
1 dsp soya bean or corn oil
3 tbsp crunchy peanut butter
2 tsp light brown sugar
1 dsp light soy sauce
50 ml / 2 fl oz skimmed milk

Preheat the grill to medium.

Using a parer, cut the carrots and courgettes down their lengths into thin ribbons and wrap these around the cubes of tofu. Quarter two of the onions.

Thread the tofu cubes and onion on kebab sticks.

Crush the garlic and mash it into the olive oil with some black pepper and a very little salt. Brush this over the kebabs and put to cook under the grill for about 10 minutes, turning several times.

Meanwhile, make the sauce: chop the remaining onion finely, heat the oil in a non-stick saucepan and sauté the chopped onion until golden. Stir in the peanut butter, sugar and soy sauce. Gradually add 100 ml / 3½ fl oz water over a medium heat, stirring. Finally mix in the milk.

When the kebabs are golden, serve them with the peanut sauce.

OPPOSITE: Mushroom Pilaff

Salads and vegetable accompaniments

Salads and vegetables are almost as versatile within the vegetarian diet as soups and starters – and even more essential. So here are plenty of ideas with which to begin.

As so many vegetarian 'main courses' already contain vegetables, vegetarians often don't pay a lot of attention to serving side salads and vegetable accompaniments. This is a pity, as lightly cooked or raw vegetables are important in the vegetarian diet for as well as being generally rich in vitamins and minerals they are the best source – apart from fresh fruit – of vitamin C in the diet. This vitamin is depleted when it is heated and cooked, especially in a casserole or baked dish that has a long cooking time. Health considerations apart, side vegetables also add variety, visual appeal and filling power for only a few extra calories.

This chapter provides both hot and cold vegetable side dishes that best complement the main courses in the previous chapter and will go well with all kinds of bakes, loaves, etc. You can create your own side salads from seasonal vegetables and herbs and, if you like, add a little fresh or dried fruit or a sprinkling of nuts or seeds. It is easy to make a side dish look and taste impressive.

However, don't turn your nose up at plainly cooked vegetables or leaf salads. If you have a rich main course, there is nothing quite so delicious as a lightly steamed, boiled or roast vegetable served with nothing more than a little black pepper or a very light drizzle of olive oil, or a freshly picked lettuce tossed with a little balsamic vinegar.

I've also given some recipes for more substantial salads suitable as a meal in themselves for a lunch or supper or, in half portions, as starters. You can even convert some of the side dishes into more hearty dishes; for instance, you could mix the Fruit Coleslaw with a handful of hazelnuts and serve this with some bread for a light lunch.

Always buy vegetables as fresh as possible, nearing their peak, store them in cool, dark conditions and never overcook them!

Aubergine and Lentil Layer (page 84);
Chicory, Orange and Date Salad (page 103)

CANTONESE NOODLE SALAD

Try white rice noodles in this dish for a change from the more commonly available wheat-based ones.

Calories per serving: 235
Saturated fat: Low
Total fat: Medium
Protein: Medium
Carbohydrate: High
Cholesterol: 25 mg
Vitamins: A, C, E
Minerals: Iron

110 g / 4 oz (dry weight) egg-thread noodles
100 g / 3½ oz mange-tout peas, topped, tailed and halved
150 g / 5½ oz fresh beansprouts
25 g / 1 oz alfalfa sprouts
6 spring onions, cut into 2 cm / ¾ in pieces
1 large red pepper, deseeded and chopped
100 g / 3½ oz Chinese leaves, sliced
100 g / 3½ oz mushrooms, sliced
for the dressing:
1 tbsp soy sauce
2 tbsp lemon juice
1 tbsp sesame seed oil
pinch of ground ginger
1 tbsp sesame seeds
1 tbsp sunflower seeds

Soak the noodles in boiling water for a few minutes and blanch the mange-tout peas for 1 minute in boiling salted water. Drain immediately.

Combine all the vegetables in a salad bowl. In another small bowl, mix together the dressing ingredients.

Drain the noodles and add them to the salad bowl together with the dressing. Stir gently to combine and serve.

HOT BABY VEGETABLES WITH RED PESTO

Calories per serving: 208
Saturated fat: High
Total fat: High
Protein: High
Carbohydrate: Medium
Cholesterol: 11 mg
Vitamins: C, A
Minerals: Potassium, Iron, Calcium

275 g / 10 oz very small new potatoes, scrubbed
225 g / 8 oz baby carrots
175 g / 6 oz baby squash
8 shallots, peeled and sliced
75 g / 3 oz baby asparagus spears, trimmed
75 g / 3 oz fine green beans, topped and tailed, or broccoli florets
1 quantity *Red Pesto Sauce* (see *Pistou* on page 53)

Cook the potatoes in boiling salted water until tender. Meanwhile, in a steamer (preferably one with compartments), steam the other vegetables for about 10 minutes, until just tender (or you could microwave them in a little water).

When the vegetables are ready, quickly toss in a serving dish with the sauce and serve.
Note: if young asparagus is too expensive, substitute mange-tout peas.

CLASSIC THREE-BEAN SALAD WITH PASTA

Calories per serving: 347
Saturated fat: Low
Total fat: Medium
Protein: High
Carbohydrate: High
Cholesterol: Nil
Vitamins: B group, C, E
Minerals: Calcium, Iron, Potassium, Magnesium

150 g / 5½ oz pasta shells
200 g / 7 oz French beans, topped and tailed
200 g / 7 oz (drained weight) canned, or pre-cooked (see pags 22–3) cannellini beans
200 g / 7 oz (drained weight) canned, or pre-cooked (see pages 22–3) red kidney beans
6 tbsp *Light Vinaigrette* (see page 124)
2 tbsp chopped fresh parsley

Boil the pasta in plenty of lightly salted water with a little oil until it is tender but still firm.

Cook the French beans in lightly salted water for a few minutes until they are tender but still crunchy.

Drain the pasta and beans and mix with the remaining ingredients in a serving bowl.
Note: this serves 4 as a lunch or 8 as a starter – in this latter case it will provide 173 calories per serving.

OPPOSITE: Cantonese Noodle Salad

GADO GADO

This warm salad from Indonesia provides one of the nicest combinations of tastes and textures I've ever enjoyed. It is a bit of an effort to put together, but well worth the trouble.

Calories per serving: 273
Saturated fat: High
Total fat: High
Protein: High
Carbohydrate: Low
Cholesterol: 250 mg
Vitamins: A, B group, C, D, E
Minerals: Iron, Potassium, Zinc,
   Magnesium, Calcium

100 g / 3½ oz Chinese leaves, torn into large pieces
225 g / 8 oz waxy potatoes, peeled, cooked until just tender and cut into bite-sized pieces
100 g / 3½ oz carrots, cut into thick strips, blanched in boiling water for 1 minute and drained immediately
100 g / 3½ oz green beans, cut in half and blanched in boiling water for 1 minute and drained immediately
½ tbsp corn oil
50 g / 2 oz cucumber, cut into thick strips
100 g / 3½ oz fresh beansprouts
4 medium eggs, hard-boiled, shelled and quartered
1 small onion, sliced and separated into rings
for the sauce:
4 tbsp coconut cream
2 tbsp smooth peanut butter
1 dsp lime juice
1 dsp light soy sauce
1 tsp Tabasco or other chilli sauce

Mix the sauce ingredients together and set aside.

Line a serving dish with the Chinese leaves and divide up the cooked vegetables between the dishes, arranging them attractively.

Heat the oil in a small non-stick frying pan and stir-fry the cucumber and beansprouts over a high heat for 1–2 minutes, until crisp. Sprinkle these on the vegetables and dot with the quartered eggs.

Add the onion to the pan and stir-fry that until it is crisp and golden. Pour the dressing over the salad and top with the onion to garnish.

The salad should still be slightly warm when served, so the vegetables are best cooked just before you arrange the salads.

PASTA WALDORF

You can serve half portions of this dish as a starter if people are very hungry, or give yourself a half portion with some bread if you're slimming. Otherwise, this is a really hearty main-course dish.

Calories per serving: 430
Saturated fat: Low
Total fat: Medium
Protein: Medium
Carbohydrate: High
Cholesterol: 5 mg
Vitamins: A, B group, D, C
Minerals: Calcium, Potassium,
   Iron

225 g / 8 oz (dry weight) pasta shells
3 small red eating apples
1 tbsp lemon juice
6 celery stalks, chopped
50 g / 2 oz walnut pieces
50 g / 2 oz sultanas
50 g / 2 oz reduced-fat Cheddar cheese, cut into small cubes
for the dressing:
1 quantity *Light Mayonnaise* (see page 124)
about 3 tbsp skimmed milk
frisée lettuce leaves, to serve (optional)
2 tbsp chopped fresh parsley, to garnish

Cook the pasta in boiling salted water until tender. Drain and let cool.

Core and deseed the apples and toss them in the lemon juice.

Combine all the salad ingredients in a salad bowl or on a platter lined with frisée lettuce leaves.

Make the dressing by adding just enough of the skimmed milk to the mayonnaise to give it a pouring consistency.

Dribble the dressing over the salad and toss lightly to ensure that all the ingredients are evenly coated. Sprinkle the parsley over to garnish.

BROWN RICE SALAD WITH MUSHROOMS AND BEANS

I prefer the nutty taste of brown rice in this salad, but you could use Basmati or even soaked bulghar wheat.

Calories per serving: 395
Saturated fat: Low
Total fat: Medium
Protein: Medium
Carbohydrate: High
Cholesterol: Nil
Vitamins: B group, C, A, E
Minerals: Iron, Potassium, Zinc

225 g / 8 oz (dry weight) brown rice, washed and drained
225 g / 8 oz (drained weight) canned or pre-cooked (see pages 22–3) cannellini beans
110 g / 4 oz each (drained weight) canned or pre-cooked (see pages 22–3) borlotti and adzuki beans
110 g / 4 oz small brown-cap mushrooms, sliced
1 medium red pepper, deseeded and chopped
2 celery stalks, chopped
50 g / 2 oz cucumber, chopped
6 spring onions, chopped
1 small red apple, chopped
4 tbsp *Light Vinaigrette* (see page 124)

Cook the rice in 700 ml / 1¼ pints boiling salted water for 30 minutes, or until tender but not soggy and all the water is absorbed (add extra water during cooking at any time if the rice dries out but still isn't tender). Allow to cool slightly.

Combine the rice with all the other ingredients in a salad bowl and serve.

AVOCADO AND LEAF SALAD

Avocados are high in fat, but quite low in saturates and high in the 'good-for-you' monounsaturates.

Calories per serving: 290
Saturated fat: Medium
Total fat: High
Protein: Medium
Carbohydrate: Low
Cholesterol: Nil
Vitamins: A, C, E
Minerals: Potassium, Iron, Calcium

1 beef tomato
450 g / 1 lb mixed salad leaves, including some dark leaves
1 bunch of watercress, trimmed and separated
4 large spring onions, chopped
2 medium-to-small ripe avocados
2 tbsp *Light Vinaigrette* (see page 124)
50 g / 2 oz pine nuts

Quarter the tomato, deseed it and roughly chop it. Put the leaves in a serving bowl with the tomato, watercress and onions.

Halve, stone and peel the avocados. Slice the flesh and add it to the salad. Immediately pour the dressing over and gently toss to combine.

Serve the salad with the pine nuts sprinkled over. This salad works well as a light lunch with sesame rolls.

APPLE, NUT AND CARROT SALAD

Calories per serving: 203
Saturated fat: Medium
Total fat: High
Protein: Medium
Carbohydrate: Low
Cholesterol: Nil
Vitamins: C, A, E
Minerals: Potassium, Iron

325 g / 12 oz carrots, peeled and grated
2 red eating apples
25 g / 1 oz cashew nuts
15 g / ½ oz sunflower seeds
15 g / ½ oz walnuts, chopped
1 tbsp lemon juice
50 g / 2 oz raisins
3 tbsp *Light Vinaigrette* (see page 124)

Core and slice the apples and sprinkle with lemon juice.

Combine all the ingredients in a salad bowl. *Note*: half portions of this salad make good side salads, while a whole portion makes a very big starter or light lunch.

PREVIOUS PAGES: Apple, Nut and Carrot Salad; Avocado and Leaf Salad

FRUIT COLESLAW

This slaw is good as part of a buffet, in sandwiches with cheese or one of the spreads on pages 63–6.

Calories per serving: 106
Saturated fat: Medium
Total fat: Medium
Protein: Medium
Carbohydrate: Medium
Cholesterol: 10 mg
Vitamins: C
Minerals: Potassium

½ small white cabbage (about 325 g / 12 oz)
110 g / 4 oz small seedless grapes
15 g / ½ oz desiccated coconut
110 g / 4 oz pineapple, cut into slices then slivers
4 tbsp *Light Mayonnaise* (see page 124)
2 tbsp low-fat natural yogurt

Slice the cabbage thinly, then chop it into 3 cm / 1¼ in lengths and put these into a salad bowl. Halve the grapes and mix them into the cabbage together with the coconut and pineapple.

Combine the light mayonnaise with the yogurt and pour this dressing over the salad. Toss lightly to combine and chill before serving.

Note: you can add extra ingredients to this salad as you fancy: eg grated carrots or onions, chopped apple or fresh apricots.

CHICORY, ORANGE AND DATE SALAD

Calories per serving: 46
Saturated fat: Low
Total fat: Low
Protein: Medium
Carbohydrate: High
Cholesterol: Nil
Vitamins: C, Folic acid
Minerals: Iron, Potassium, Calcium

2 heads of chicory, sliced
1 large orange
50 g / 2 oz stoned dried dates, chopped
3 tbsp oil-free French dressing

Peel the orange, removing all the pith. Segment it with a sharp serrated knife.

Mix all the ingredients together in a salad bowl. This goes well with cheese and any bake or nut loaf.

Note: you can use 75 g / 3 oz fresh dates instead, which will provide a slightly different texture. You can also vary the salad by using the oil-free Vinegar Dressing on page 125.

WINTER RED SALAD

Calories per serving: 110
Saturated fat: High
Total fat: High
Protein: Medium
Carbohydrate: Low
Cholesterol: Nil
Vitamins: A, C, Folic acid
Minerals: Potassium

1 oak leaf lettuce (about 100 g / 3½ oz)
1 head of radicchio
150 g / 5½ oz cooked beetroot, peeled and diced
1 red onion, thinly sliced
100 g / 3½ oz red cabbage, shredded
4 tbsp *Light Vinaigrette* (see page 124)
7 g / ¼ oz sesame seeds

Separate the lettuce and radicchio into leaves and tear the bigger ones. Carefully clean and dry the leaves if necessary.

Put all ingredients except the seeds in a salad bowl and toss lightly. Garnish with the seeds.

Note: this salad looks very pretty and goes well with all kinds of cheese.

ORANGE AND WATERCRESS SALAD

Calories per serving: 53
Saturated fat: Low
Total fat: Low
Protein: Low
Carbohydrate: High
Cholesterol: Nil
Vitamins: C, A
Minerals: Iron, Potassium

1 bunch of watercress, trimmed
2 oranges, peeled, pith removed and thinly sliced into rounds
50 g / 2 oz dried apricots, chopped
1 tbsp lemon juice
1 level tsp lemon grass, soaked and drained if not using fresh
sprigs of fresh herbs, to garnish

Arrange the watercress on the base of a shallow serving bowl.

Arrange the orange slices and apricots on top and sprinkle with the lemon juice and lemon grass.

Garnish with a few sprigs of fresh herbs.

Note: this tangy salad is excellent with any rich cake, pie or loaf.

GUMBO CREOLE

Use as a side vegetable, or add some cubes of tofu and serve with a grain or pasta for a main meal.

Calories per serving: 86
Saturated fat: Medium
Total fat: High
Protein: High
Carbohydrate: Medium
Cholesterol: Nil
Vitamins: A, C, Folic acid, E
Minerals: Iron, Potassium,
    Calcium, Magnesium

1 tbsp sunflower oil
1 medium onion, chopped
225 g / 8 oz okra, trimmed and
    chopped in half
1 red and 1 green pepper, deseeded
    and sliced
1 celery stalk, chopped
one 400 g / 14 oz can chopped
    tomatoes
1 tbsp tomato purée
275 ml / ½ pint *Vegetable Stock*
    (see page 122)
½ tsp chilli powder
salt and black pepper

Heat the oil in a heavy medium flameproof casserole dish. Sauté the onion in it gently for 5 minutes. Add the okra and peppers and sauté for a further 10 minutes. Add the celery and stir for a minute. Stir in the tomatoes and tomato purée.

Add the stock and chilli powder. Bring to a simmer, reduce the heat and cover. Simmer for 45 minutes, or until the okra is tender and the gumbo is thick.

Season to taste before serving.

LEMON AND GARLIC ROAST POTATOES

Cook these in the oven with any bake or loaf.

Calories per serving: 225
Saturated fat: Low
Total fat: Low
Protein: Medium
Carbohydrate: High
Cholesterol: Nil
Vitamins: C
Minerals: Potassium

900 g / 2 lb new potatoes, scrubbed
2 large garlic cloves, chopped
juice of ½ lemon
1 tbsp olive oil
1 tbsp chopped thyme
salt and black pepper
thyme sprigs and strips of lemon peel
    to garnish (optional)

Preheat the oven to 200°C / 400°F / gas6.

Cut larger potatoes into fairly small chunks and toss with the rest of the ingredients.

Spread them out on a roasting pan and pour over any remaining juices. Roast for 45 minutes, turning and basting once or twice.

Garnish with thyme sprigs and strips of lemon peel, if using.

Note: instead of adding the garlic chopped, try roasting some whole unpeeled garlic cloves with the potatoes to squeeze over them at the table.

FRIED PEPPERS WITH TOMATO AND GARLIC

These are lovely with any egg dish. Mixed with grated cheese, they also make a good quick supper.

Calories per serving: 65
Saturated fat: Medium
Total fat: High
Protein: Medium
Carbohydrate: Nil
Cholesterol: 10 mg
Vitamins: A, C, E
Minerals: Potassium

1 tbsp olive oil
1 medium onion, finely chopped
1 large garlic clove, chopped
1 large red and 1 large green pepper,
    deseeded and thinly sliced
1 dsp chopped oregano
275 g / 10 oz canned chopped
    tomatoes (with their liquid)
salt and black pepper

Heat the oil in a non-stick frying pan and sauté the onion over a medium heat until soft and just turning golden.

Stir in the garlic and peppers and fry for 15 more minutes, adding a little juice from the tomatoes if necessary.

Add the oregano, tomatoes and seasoning. Cover and simmer for 10 minutes, stirring once or twice.

Note: you can leave this to simmer very gently for much longer if you have the time – it seems to improve the flavour even further.

OPPOSITE: Lemon and Garlic Roast Potatoes

Sweet treats and breakfasts

Desserts, cakes, cookies, scones and muffins are just some of the indulgences you can enjoy without feeling guilty by means of the reduced-fat, reduced-sugar recipes in this chapter.

Many a vegetarian's downfall in the quest for a healthy diet is a sweet tooth – which will never quite be satisfied by fresh fruit.

There are two ways of fitting desserts into a healthy and non-fattening diet. One is to exercise extreme restraint in both portion-size and frequency – which is fine if you can do it. The other is to find ways to produce results just as tempting as the high-calorie equivalents, but which contain less fat, less sugar and fewer calories.

One of the best ways to reduce sugar content is to make use of fruit's own natural sweetness (as in, say, the Peach and Raisin Cookies on page 111) so that added sugar can be reduced. I have also substituted fructose (fruit sugar) for ordinary sugar where appropriate, as it is twice as sweet for the same number of calories.

The last reason you mustn't feel guilty about indulging in my sweets is that they are all rich in vitamins and minerals – and most contain a lot of fibre.

When making your own desserts, remember that those based on fruit are preferable to heavy puddings and pastries. However, if you do like a 'real' pudding, bread is a better bet than pastry – summer puddings and charlottes made with all kinds of fruit fillings are delicious, filling and healthy. Filo is another good choice, as it is far less calorific than other pastries. Use the Filo Tarts recipe on page 90 and fill them with chopped fresh fruit and fromage frais, then drizzle a little honey over.

Breakfast can also be a happy blend of indulging a sweet tooth and getting a really healthy start to the day. All the breakfast recipes here achieve that – and for more healthy morning meal ideas, turn to the diet plans starting on pages 35 and 45.

Summer Pudding (page 108)

SUMMER PUDDING

This tastes deceptively wicked, but it is actually a vitamin- and fibre-rich low-fat wonder! It is really nice served with Greek-style yogurt or crème fraîche.

Calories per serving: 180 to serve 4; 120 to serve 6
Saturated fat: Low
Total fat: Low
Protein: Medium
Carbohydrate: High
Cholesterol: Nil
Vitamins: C
Minerals: Iron, Calcium

900 g / 2 lb mixed soft fruits (eg raspberries, blackberries and redcurrants), hulled
about 40 g / 1½ oz fructose
6 large slices of bread (white or wholemeal), crusts removed (about 175 g / 6 oz)

Put all the fruits in a saucepan with a very little water and the fructose. Bring slowly to a simmer, remove from the heat and adjust sweetness if necessary.

Line a 1.1 litre / 2 pint pudding basin carefully with most of the bread, making sure there are no gaps. Fill the lined basin with the fruit and most of the juice. Top with the rest of the bread to cover completely, trimming as necessary.

Put a plate on top of the pudding and a heavy weight on top of that. Put the basin on a large plate (because some juices will probably run out of the basin). Leave overnight in the fridge. Keep the remaining juice in a jug in the fridge.

When ready to serve, remove the weight and covering plate and slide a spatula around the inside of the basin to release the pudding. Turn out on a serving plate, cut the pudding into slices with a carving knife and pour the extra juice over.

BAKED BANANAS WITH LEMON AND ORANGE

Calories per serving: 110
Saturated fat: Nil
Total fat: Low
Protein: Low
Carbohydrate: High
Cholesterol: Nil
Vitamins: C, Folic acid
Minerals: Potassium

4 bananas
juice of 1 lemon
juice of 1 orange, plus 4 slices of orange, peeled and trimmed with a knife
1 tbsp dark brown sugar

Preheat the oven to 180°C / 350°F / gas4.

Peel the bananas and arrange them on 4 pieces of foil large enough to wrap the bananas comfortably. Sprinkle with the citrus juices and sugar and top with an orange slice.

Wrap the foil in loose parcels and tightly seal the edges. Bake for 20 minutes.

Serve the bananas in the foil parcels.

BAKED PEACHES

Calories per serving: 93
Saturated fat: High
Total fat: Medium
Protein: Low
Carbohydrate: High
Cholesterol: 8 mg
Vitamins: C
Minerals: Trace

4 ripe peaches
1 tbsp brown sugar
1 tbsp lemon juice
15 g / ½ oz butter or vegetarian
   margarine

Preheat the oven to 180°C / 350°F / gas4.
   Cut off a thin layer of flesh from the top and bottom of the peaches and sit them on a baking dish. Sprinkle the sugar and lemon juice over them, dot with butter and bake for 20 minutes.
Note: these are lovely with vanilla ice-cream.

CARIBBEAN TEACAKE

You won't keep this around for long once it's made, and it is so good for you it is almost saintly!

Makes about 18 slices
Calories per 50 g / 2 oz slice: 155
Saturated fat: Low
Total fat: High
Protein: Medium
Carbohydrate: Medium
Cholesterol: 27 mg per slice
Vitamins: A, B group, D, E
Minerals: Iron, Potassium,
   Magnesium, Zinc

200 g / 7 oz sweet potato (the orange-fleshed variety, not the watery white-fleshed one), peeled and cubed
175 g / 6 oz soft dark brown sugar
125 g / 4½ oz plain wholemeal flour, sifted
pinch of ground cinnamon
1 level tsp grated nutmeg
75 ml / 3 fl oz sunflower oil
2 medium eggs, separated
1 level tsp bicarbonate of soda mixed with 3 tbsp water
½ tsp vanilla essence
75 g / 3 oz chopped almonds
50 g / 2 oz desiccated coconut

Preheat the oven to 180°C / 350°F / gas4.
   Boil the sweet potato in a very little water until tender (about 10 minutes). Add half of the sugar (without draining any surplus water away) and purée. Reserve.
   In a large bowl, combine the flour, remaining sugar, cinnamon and nutmeg. Make a well in the centre and stir in the oil, egg yolks, bicarbonate mixture and vanilla. Fold in the nuts, sweet potato and the coconut.
   Beat the egg whites until they form stiff peaks and fold into the mixture.
   Pack into a 900 g / 2 lb non-stick loaf tin and bake for 1¼ hours or until cooked.
   Allow to cool slightly, turn out on a rack and let cool completely.

REDUCED-FAT SCONES

Those of you with a sweet tooth can eat these scones without feeling guilty.

Makes 8
Calories per scone: 150
Saturated fat: Medium
Total fat: Medium
Protein: Medium
Carbohydrate: High
Cholesterol: Not known
Vitamins: B group
Minerals: Zinc

175 g / 6 oz plain wholemeal flour
50 g / 2 oz plain white flour
1 tbsp baking powder
little salt
50 g / 2 oz caster sugar
50 g / 2 oz reduced-fat cooking spread
75 ml / 3 fl oz skimmed milk

Preheat the oven to 200°C / 400°F / gas6 with a non-stick baking sheet in it.
   Sift the flours, baking powder and salt into a mixing bowl and tip any wholemeal flour left in the sieve into the mixing bowl.
   Add the sugar and stir in. Rub the fat into the flour lightly with your fingertips, until the mixture resembles fine breadcrumbs. Add the milk to make a dough that comes away cleanly from the sides of the bowl.
   Either cut 8 rounds from the rolled-out dough or form it into a 15 cm / 6 in round and mark that into 8 triangles. Put on the preheated baking sheet and bake for 15 minutes.

LEMON AND LIME SORBET

This is a really easy and refreshing dessert.

Calories per serving: 162
Saturated fat: Low
Total fat: Low
Protein: Low
Carbohydrate: High
Cholesterol: Nil
Vitamins: C
Minerals: Trace

150 g / 5½ oz caster sugar
100 ml / 3½ fl oz fresh lemon juice
100 ml / 3½ fl oz fresh lime juice
whites of 2 eggs

Dissolve the sugar in 350 ml / 12½ fl oz water over a low heat, stirring. Bring to the boil and boil for 10 minutes. Let cool.

Add the lemon and lime juices, pour the mixture into a plastic dish and freeze until mushy. Turn out into a large mixing bowl and whisk until frothy.

In another bowl beat the egg whites until they form stiff peaks and fold them into the juice mixture. Put back in the plastic dish and freeze until firm.

Pop in the fridge for a few minutes before eating, to allow to soften up slightly.

HAZELNUT ICE-CREAM

This is an easy way to enliven vanilla ice-cream.

Calories per serving: 160
Saturated fat: Medium
Total fat: Medium
Protein: Medium
Carbohydrate: Low
Cholesterol: Nil
Vitamins: B
Minerals: Iron, Calcium

40 g / 1½ oz stale wholemeal breadcrumbs
40 g / 1½ oz brown sugar
20 g / ¾ oz shelled roasted hazelnuts, finely chopped
1 level tsp ground cinnamon
½ tsp ground mixed spice
400 ml / 14 fl oz low-calorie vanilla ice-cream, slightly softened

Preheat the oven to 190°C / 375°F / gas5.

Combine the breadcrumbs, sugar and nuts and spread the mixture out on a baking tray. Bake for 5–10 minutes, until crunchy (check from time to time, as the mixture is easily burnt.)

Remove from the oven and mix in the spices. Then quickly fold the mixture into the ice-cream, return the ice-cream to a plastic container and freeze briefly to firm it up again.

PEACH AND RAISIN COOKIES

This American-style cookie is a sort of cross between a cake and a biscuit. They shouldn't be stored with other biscuits as they will make them go soft.

Makes 20 big cookies
Calories per cookie: 145
Saturated fat: Medium
Total fat: Medium
Protein: High
Carbohydrate: High
Cholesterol: 12 mg per cookie
Vitamins: A, Folic acid, D
Minerals: Iron, Potassium, Calcium, Zinc

250 g / 9 oz plain wholemeal flour
1 tsp salt
1 tsp baking powder
pinch of bicarbonate of soda
½ tsp ground cinnamon
25 g / 1 oz rolled oats
110 g / 4 oz reduced-fat cooking spread
225 g / 8 oz soft light brown sugar
1 egg, beaten
140 ml / 5 fl oz skimmed milk
100 g / 3½ oz dried peaches, chopped
100 g / 3½ oz raisins
2 tsp finely grated orange zest

Preheat the oven to 200°C / 400°F / gas6.

Sift the flour, salt, baking powder, bicarbonate and cinnamon together into a mixing bowl, and tip any bits of flour left in the sieve into the bowl. Add the oats and stir.

Cream the fat and sugar in another bowl. Beat the egg with the milk.

Add these dry and wet ingredient mixtures alternately to the fat and sugar mixture, stirring each addition in well. Finally add the peaches, raisins and orange zest.

Put the mixture one tablespoon at a time on a non-stick baking sheet, allowing at least 2–3 cm / ¾–1¼ in between spoonfuls. Bake for 15 minutes. Allow to cool and then store in an airtight container.

MARINATED STRAWBERRIES

Serve this easy dessert or breakfast with fromage frais, low-fat yogurt or – for a special treat – thick Greek-style yogurt.

Calories per serving: 55
Saturated fat: Nil
Total fat: Low
Protein: Low
Carbohydrate; High
Cholesterol: Nil
Vitamins: C
Minerals: Potassium

450 g / 1 lb ripe strawberries, hulled
juice of 1 large orange
juice of 1 lime, plus lime slices
1 level tbsp fructose
1 level tsp arrowroot, blended with
    2 tsp cold water
mint leaves, to garnish

Halve all but 4 of the strawberries. Put the strawberry halves and whole strawberries in a shallow bowl.

Mix the citrus juices and fructose with 75 ml / 3 fl oz water. Pour over the strawberries and leave in the fridge to marinate for about 30 minutes, turning the strawberries once.

Drain the marinade into a small saucepan, add the arrowroot mixture and stir over a medium heat until the mixture bubbles and thickens.

Arrange the strawberry halves in 4 serving dishes and pour the sauce over. Garnish each with a whole strawberry and some mint leaves.

BANANA AND WALNUT TEABREAD

Makes about 12 slices
Calories per slice: 115
Saturated fat: Medium
Total fat: High
Protein: Medium
Carbohydrate: Medium
Cholesterol: 4 mg per slice
Vitamins: A, B, D
Minerals: Iron

50 g / 2 oz vegetarian margarine
50 g / 2 oz soft dark brown sugar
1 medium banana
2 eggs, beaten
110 g / 4 oz wholemeal flour
1 medium carrot, peeled, chopped and
    puréed in blender or very finely
    grated
25 g / 1 oz chopped walnuts

Preheat the oven to 180°C / 350°F / gas4.

In a mixing bowl, blend together the margarine and sugar until creamy. Mash the banana and blend this into the mixture.

Add the egg little by little (to prevent curdling, add a very little flour as you beat in the egg). Add the carrot and nuts and mix well. Add the rest of the flour.

Spread the mixture evenly into a 450 g / 1 lb non-stick loaf tin and bake for 30 minutes. Allow to cool on a rack.

PINEAPPLE MUFFINS

These American-style muffins make a quick breakfast.

Makes 8
Calories per serving: 185
Saturated fat: Medium
Total fat: Medium
Protein: Medium
Carbohydrate: High
Cholesterol: Not known
Vitamins: A, D, E
Minerals: Iron, Potassium,
    Calcium

225 g / 8 oz wholemeal self-raising
    flour
pinch of salt
1 medium eating apple
100 g / 3½ oz pineapple, chopped
    small
150 ml / 5½ fl oz skimmed milk
50 g / 2 oz reduced-fat cooking
    spread, diced
50 g / 2 oz brown sugar
2 medium eggs, beaten

Preheat the oven to 190°C / 375°F / gas5.

Sift the flour and salt into a mixing bowl and tip any flour left in the sieve into the bowl. Peel, core and grate the apple.

Stir all the ingredients into the flour gradually until you have a smooth mixture. Pour into muffin tins and bake for 20–25 minutes.

Allow to cool slightly before turning out on a wire rack to cool completely.

OPPOSITE: Marinated Strawberries; Banana and Walnut Teabread

APRICOT AND BRANDY SPREAD

The brandy in this spread is not just there to give a luxurious taste for a few calories – it helps to preserve the spread, which will keep for a week or two in an airtight container in the fridge.

Calories per serving: 77
Saturated fat: Low
Total fat: Low
Protein: Medium
Carbohydrate: High
Cholesterol: Nil
Vitamins: A, B2
Minerals: Magnesium, Iron, Calcium

100 g / 3½ oz dried apricots, chopped
25 g / 1 oz sultanas
1 tbsp honey
1 tbsp brandy

Put the apricots in a saucepan with 200 ml / 7 fl oz water and bring to the boil. Simmer and remove any scum that rises.

After 5 minutes, add the sultanas and honey. As the mixture thickens, add the brandy and simmer for a further 3 minutes.

Let cool and put through the blender.
Note: this quantity gives four very generous servings.

BANANA SPREAD

Calories per serving: 112
Saturated fat: Low
Total fat: Medium
Protein: Medium
Carbohydrate: High
Cholesterol: Nil
Vitamins: A, C
Minerals: Potassium

3 medium bananas
1 dsp lemon juice
30 g / 1¼ oz ground almonds
1 dsp soft brown sugar

Peel the bananas and mash them in a bowl with the lemon juice. Add the almonds and sugar and blend thoroughly.

This makes a good sandwich filling, or a sweet dip for strawberries or slices of apple.
Note: if you like you can use flaked almonds and put the mixture through an electric blender for a few seconds.

SCOTTISH OATCAKES

These go well with a variety of things, so make a good portable snack or breakfast.

Makes 18
Calories per oatcake: 78
Saturated fat: Medium
Total fat: High
Protein: Medium
Carbohydrate: High
Cholesterol: Nil
Vitamins: B group, A
Minerals: Iron, Potassium

225 g / 8 oz rolled porridge oats
50 g / 2 oz wholemeal flour
1 tsp baking powder
50 g / 2 oz polyunsaturated margarine
little salt
little boiling water
little flour for dusting

Preheat the oven to 190°C / 375°F / gas5.

Mix the oats, flour and baking powder in a mixing bowl. Melt the margarine and stir this into the mixture. Slowly add a little boiling water, until you have a workable dough.

Knead gently on a floured surface, until the dough is pliable and soft. Roll out to a thickness of about 3 mm / ⅛ in. Cut out 18 rounds using a cookie cutter and put on a non-stick baking tray.

Bake for 10–15 minutes .
Note: triangles are a traditional oatcake shape, so roll the dough into two or three rounds and cut these across to make triangular wedges, if you prefer.

OPPOSITE: Apricot and Brandy Spread

FRUIT COMPOTE

You can vary the fruits in this to suit yourself. If the compote is going to be served within a day or so you can even add fresh fruits for a change.

Calories per serving: 248
Saturated fat: Low
Total fat: Low
Protein: Low
Carbohydrate: High
Cholesterol: Nil
Vitamins: Folic acid
Minerals: Iron, Potassium

50 g / 2 oz dried pears and stoned prunes
100 g / 3½ oz each dried peaches and apple rings
25 g / 1 oz each dried banana flakes and sultanas
350 ml / 12½ fl oz orange juice
3 whole cloves
1 small piece of cinnamon stick
1 tsp grated lemon zest
pinch of ground ginger

Place all the ingredients in a saucepan with 100 ml / 3½ fl oz water, bring to a simmer and cook for 20–40 minutes, or until all the fruits are very tender (this varies greatly so check after 20 minutes).

Serve hot or cold.

Note: this will keep several days, covered, in the fridge.

AMERICAN-STYLE GRANOLA

This granola is higher in fat and calories than muesli, but it is delicious sprinkled on yogurt and fruits or used as a crumble topping for fruit.

Makes twelve 25 g / 1 oz servings
Calories per serving: 124
Saturated fat: Low
Total fat: High
Protein: Medium
Carbohydrate: Medium
Cholesterol: Nil
Vitamins: Folic acid, E
Minerals: Iron, Potassium

15 g / ½ oz sunflower oil
15 g / ½ oz runny honey
175 g / 6 oz rolled oats
25 g / 1 oz each whole-wheat flakes, sesame seeds, sunflower seeds and mixed chopped nuts
1 tsp ground cinnamon

Preheat the oven to 160°C / 325°F / gas3. Combine the oil and honey and mix with the other ingredients. Spread this out evenly on a non-stick baking tray and bake for about 30 minutes, turning once. Check regularly to ensure it isn't over-browning.

Remove from the oven when deep golden brown.

SPECIAL RECIPE MUESLI

Makes eight 75 g / 3 oz servings
Calories per serving: 297
Saturated fat: Low
Total fat: Medium
Protein: Medium
Carbohydrate: High
Cholesterol: Nil
Vitamins: E, B group
Minerals: Iron, Calcium, Potassium, Magnesium

325 g / 12 oz rolled oats, or mixture of rolled grains of choice
25 g / 1 oz crushed bran flakes
50 g / 2 oz each raisins, chopped no-soak dried apricots and chopped no-soak dried peaches
25 g / 1 oz each sunflower seeds, hazelnuts, cashew nuts and chopped stoned dates
15 g / ½ oz each sesame seeds and wheatgerm

Mix all ingredients in a large bowl and store in an airtight container.

Note: you can vary the proportions – and, indeed, the types of nuts and fruits – to suit yourself, but bear in mind that if you increase the nut and seed content significantly you will also increase the fat and calorie content.

OPPOSITE: Fruit Compote; American-style Granola

Basic recipes

Of course you can go out and buy all the basics you need for your cooking – from yogurt to pizza bases and pastry. Usually, however, it is healthier – and more fun – to make your own!

From time to time, everyone falls back on buying 'basics'. As we are all so busy, this is nothing to feel ashamed about. There are some highly acceptable basics on the market, from ready-made tomato sauces and mayonnaise to pastas.

There are, in fact, a few basics that it is hardly worth the bother of making yourself. Bread making, for example, is quite time-consuming and not everyone seems to have the gift for it – so why worry, when nowadays there is such a plentiful and varied supply of good breads in most areas – from Mediterranean varieties to organic loaves.

There are, however, some things that do seem always to taste better if you make them yourself. For instance it is hard to get a good bought wholemeal pastry or pancake, good vegetable stock is rare, and so is a good spice blend for curry.

Other ready-made products may seem quite acceptable, but they often have a high additive content. So I've selected several basic recipes that I think you will find most useful. I've included yogurt because, although you can find good yogurt in the shops, if – like me – you eat a lot of it, it can work out quite expensive. It is easy, quick and inexpensive to make your own.

Pancakes, pastry and pizza bases can all be frozen, as can the vegetable stock (reduce it first to save storage space). The curry blend will keep for a while in an opaque airtight jar, or in a glass jar kept in cool dark conditions.

Dressings will keep for a few days in the fridge. You can use the basic dressing recipes with your own variations – added spices and herbs etc. You can also make a very simple dressing by mixing natural yogurt with lemon juice and seasonings. Most commercial dressings are quite high in fat, so it really is worth having a good repertoire that you can produce at home in a few shakes.

Pizza Base (page 121); Wholemeal Shortcrust Pastry (page 120)   119

WHOLEMEAL SHORTCRUST PASTRY

This quantity makes enough for a 20 cm / 8 in flan or pie crust to serve four.

Calories per serving: 145
Saturated fat: High
Total fat: High
Protein: Medium
Carbohydrate: Medium
Cholesterol: Not known
Vitamins: Folic acid, A, D
Minerals: Iron, Potassium

100 g / 3½ oz wholemeal flour
½ tsp baking powder
pinch of salt
50 g / 2 oz reduced-fat cooking block
2–3 tbsp cold water

Sieve the flour, baking powder and salt into a mixing bowl, returning any flour left in the sieve to the bowl.

Put the fat into the mixing bowl and cut it into pieces with a sharp knife. Then, using light fingers, rub the fat into the flour until the mixture resembles breadcrumbs.

Sprinkle on 2 tablespoons of the cold water and draw the dough together with a spatula, adding a little more water if necessary until the dough comes away cleanly from the sides of the bowl. (Whatever you do, don't add too much water or you will spoil the pastry.)

Cover the pastry with foil and let it sit in the fridge for 30 minutes.

Lightly flour a pastry board or suitable surface and the rolling pin. Make the pastry into a flattish, even round and roll the pastry out evenly and carefully, giving it a one-quarter turn or so between rollings, until you have a very thin sheet.

(If at any time the pastry looks like sticking to the board, lift it using the rolling pin and add more flour underneath and more flour to the rolling pin. If the pastry splits, stick it back together!)

Trim the pastry to size before using it to line the flan tin or cover the pie. (To prevent the pastry breaking, lift it using the rolling pin.)

EGG PASTA

Making pasta is quite easy, but my home-made version is not suitable for vegans as I find a home-made version without eggs is always disappointing.

Makes 4 very generous servings
Calories per serving: 360
Saturated fat: Low
Total fat: Low
Protein: Medium
Carbohydrate: High
Cholesterol: 187 mg
Vitamins: A, B group, D, E
Minerals: Calcium, Iron

325 g / 12 oz plain white flour
generous pinch of salt
3 medium eggs
1 dsp olive oil

Make sure your work surface is very clean and dry and after weighing the flour put it straight on the surface. Sprinkle on the salt.

Make a well in the centre and break the eggs into it. Pour in the oil and, using your fingers, gradually work the eggs and flour together until you have a dough.

Knead the dough for 10 minutes, until it is soft and pliable and smooth. Roll it out as thinly as you can and then cut it into thin ribbons.

Cook the pasta in plenty of boiling salted water for about 3 minutes.

PIZZA BASE

You can buy ready-made pizza bases and some are quite good, but if you have a spare few minutes it is fun to make your own. You can make the pizza using wholemeal flour. You can also put an egg into the mixture for a richer dough, but I prefer the non-egg version.

Calories per serving: 315
   (one-quarter of the base)
Saturated fat: Low
Total fat: Low
Protein: Medium
Carbohydrate: High
Cholesterol: Nil
Vitamins: Trace
Minerals: Calcium

325 g / 12 oz strong plain flour
1 tsp salt
1 tsp dried yeast
175 ml / 6 fl oz hand-hot water
1 tbsp olive oil

Sieve the flour and salt into a large bowl. In a small bowl, whisk the yeast with the sugar and a little of the water. Leave until frothy, and then pour into the large bowl with the remaining water and oil.

Mix to a soft dough, adding a little more water if necessary, until the dough comes away cleanly from the bowl.

Knead the dough for about 10 minutes on a lightly floured smooth surface. Place in a lightly oiled bowl, cover and stand in a warm place for 45 minutes, or until doubled in size.

Oil a 30 cm / 12 in pizza tin and press the dough in it to fit. Add a half quantity (or as much as you can get on) of Tomato Sauce (see page 69) plus your favourite topping and bake in an oven preheated to 200°C / 400°F / gas6 for 25 minutes.

Note: if you don't have a pizza pan you can place the pizza on a baking sheet.

PANCAKES

* *Fill with lightly cooked asparagus spears and top with* Cheese Sauce *(page 67).*
* *Fill with the* Crispy Vegetable Pie *filling (page 86) and grate cheese over the top before baking.*
* *Fill sweet pancakes with chopped banana and brown sugar and top with puréed raspberries or apricots.*

Makes 8
Calories per serving (2 pancakes):
   157
Saturated fat: Low
Total fat: Medium
Protein: High
Carbohydrate: High
Cholesterol: 63 mg
Vitamins: A, B, D, E
Minerals: Calcium, Iron

110 g / 4 oz plain flour (or use whole-wheat, or a mixture of equal parts buckwheat and whole-wheat for French crêpes)
pinch of salt
1 medium egg
250 ml / ½ pint skimmed milk
little caster sugar to taste (for sweet pancakes)
1 dsp corn oil

Sieve the flour and salt into a mixing bowl. Make a well in the centre and add the egg. Gradually beat it in with little bits of the flour. Gradually add the milk as you do this and beat until you have a smooth batter. (You could do all this in a blender.) Add sugar, if using.

You can leave this mixture to stand until you are ready to use it; it won't come to any harm.

When ready to make the pancakes, brush the base of a small non-stick frying pan with a little of the oil (which you should put in a saucer) and heat the pan well until you can feel the heat coming off the base.

Pour in just enough batter to coat the base and swirl around to make a thin pancake. Cook until the base is golden (slip a spatula under to see), turn and cook the other side for 30 seconds.

Transfer to a warm plate and keep warm, if necessary, while you make the rest.

Fill the pancakes as required (see left).

VEGETABLE STOCK

This stock will form the basis of many soups and casseroles and is added to many other dishes, too. It is worth the effort of making it, as good ready-made stock is hard to find and stock cubes are not always brilliant.

Calories for the whole amount:
  about 75
Saturated fat: Low
Total fat: Low
Protein: Low
Carbohydrate: High
Cholesterol: Nil
Vitamins: C
Minerals: Potassium

1 large onion
2 medium carrots
2 large celery stalks
1 large leek
1 green pepper, deseeded
fresh thyme
fresh parsley
12 black peppercorns
zest of 1 lemon

Chop the vegetables reasonably small and put them in a saucepan with all the other ingredients and 1 litre / 1¾ pints water.

Bring to the boil and remove any scum. Cover and simmer for 45 minutes. Allow to cool slightly and strain through a sieve, pressing the vegetables down to extract as much of the flavour and goodness as you can.

Store in the fridge and use as needed. It will keep for a few days, or will freeze.

＊ Don't use potatoes or cabbage in stock, but you can use vegetables other than the ones listed – experiment and see how you get on.

＊ You can reduce the strained stock for a fuller flavour by simmering, uncovered, until it is the strength you require.

＊ Don't add salt because not all recipes require a salted stock, you may want to reduce it down, and you can always add it later.

CURRY POWDER

Calories per tablespoon:
  approximately 10
Saturated fat: Low
Total fat: Low
Protein: Low
Carbohydrate: High
Cholesterol: Nil
Vitamins: Trace
Minerals: Iron

1 tbsp cardamom pods
1 tbsp dried red chillies, deseeded
1 tbsp cloves
8 tbsp coriander seeds
1 tbsp ground ginger (ground yourself
  from a knob of dried root ginger)
10 tbsp ground turmeric
1 tbsp black peppercorns

First get the seeds out of the cardamom pods, using a rolling pin to crush the pods. Then grind each of the whole items individually in a small electric grinder. Thoroughly combine all the ingredients and use as required. It will keep quite well in an airtight jar for a couple of months before beginning to lose its bite. *Note*: this makes a rich – but not too hot – curry; for a hotter powder, include chilli seeds.

YOGURT

Serves 4
Calories per (140 ml / 5 fl oz)
  serving: 67
Saturated fat: Low
Total fat: Low
Protein: High
Carbohydrate: Medium
Cholesterol: 4 mg
Vitamins: Niacin, A
Minerals: Calcium

2 level tbsp skimmed milk powder
550 ml / 1 pint skimmed milk
1 tbsp live natural yogurt

Dissolve the milk powder in the milk and simmer for a few minutes. Pour into a heatproof bowl and allow to cool to body temperature. Add the yogurt and stir well. Pour into a wide-necked vacuum flask and leave in a warm place for 5–6 hours.

When set, pour off and discard the whey that will be on top and put in the fridge. *Note*: the fresher your yogurt starter, the better the result – if you use old yogurt you may get a bitter taste. Also, don't leave the yogurt in the vacuum flask longer than is necessary for it to set.

OPPOSITE: Vegetable Stock ingredients

LIGHT MAYONNAISE

This is a perfectly acceptable mayonnaise-style dressing which has only one-quarter of the calories of traditional mayonnaise. You will probably also find its lighter, tangier taste preferable in salads.

Makes 8 level tbsp
Calories per level tbsp: 25
Saturated fat: Medium
Total fat: High
Protein: Medium
Carbohydrate: Low
Cholesterol: 10 mg per level tbsp
Vitamins: Trace
Minerals: Trace

2 heaped tbsp natural low-fat yogurt
3 tbsp reduced-calorie mayonnaise
1 dsp fresh lemon juice
pinch of dry mustard powder or
   turmeric
salt and black pepper

Blend all the ingredients together in a small bowl.

Stored in a screw-top container in the fridge, it will keep for at least a week.
Variations: for a sweeter taste, add a pinch of caster sugar; for a seafood dressing, add tomato purée and paprika; for a spicy dressing, add 1 tablespoon of curry powder, for a green dressing, add 1 teaspoon or more of chopped fresh leafy herbs, such as parsley, chives or chervil.

TOFU MAYONNAISE

This mayonnaise-style dressing is useful for vegans and is quite creamy and delicious.

Makes 4 tablespoons
Calories per tbsp: 35
Saturated fat: High
Total fat: High
Protein: Medium
Carbohydrate: Low
Cholesterol: Nil
Vitamins: E
Minerals: Calcium

50 g / 2 oz silken tofu
1 tbsp sunflower oil
½ tsp Dijon mustard
1 tsp lemon juice
black pepper

Put all the ingredients except the pepper in the blender and blend. Add some pepper to taste and turn out into a small lidded container.

Refrigerated, it will keep for a few days.
Variations: add garlic purée for more bite; add a pinch of saffron powder soaked in a tiny drop of water for a more Mediterranean-style dressing; add a few drops of Tabasco or other hot pepper sauce for a Mexican dip.

LIGHT VINAIGRETTE

Makes about 200 ml / 7 fl oz
Calories per tbsp: 71
Saturated fat: High
Total fat: High
Protein: Trace
Carbohydrate: Trace
Cholesterol: Nil
Vitamins: Trace
Minerals: Trace

125 ml / 4½ fl oz (8 tbsp) extra virgin
   olive oil
2 tbsp red or white wine vinegar
1 garlic clove, crushed
1 level tbsp Dijon mustard
3 tbsp cold water
salt and black pepper

Put all the ingredients in a screw-top jar and shake well or mix in a blender.

Always shake this dressing well before use. Keep it in a corked bottle in the fridge and use within 1 month.
Note: if you like you can add chopped herbs, such as a tablespoon of chopped tarragon or thyme or rosemary.

OIL-FREE VINEGAR DRESSING

Calories per serving: Trace
Saturated fat: Nil
Total fat: Nil
Protein: Trace
Carbohydrate: Trace
Cholesterol: Nil
Vitamins: Nil
Minerals: Nil

6 parts water
2 parts white wine vinegar
1 part balsamic vinegar
salt and black pepper

Blend all the ingredients together.

You can add herbs, garlic or mustard to this dressing to vary its flavour.

Note: this tangy dressing is good with all leaf salads.

JUICE DRESSING

This makes a nice change from vinaigrette on all kinds of salads and it also makes a good marinade – eg for tofu – particularly with the addition of spices.

Makes enough for 4
Calories per serving: 64
Saturated fat: High
Total fat: High
Protein: Trace
Carbohydrate: Low
Cholesterol: Nil
Vitamins: C, E
Minerals: Trace

2 tbsp extra virgin olive oil
1 tbsp each fresh orange, lemon and
   lime juice
salt and black pepper

Put all the ingredients in a screw-top jar or blender and combine well.

Refrigerate in an airtight jar or bottle until needed.

Variations: add 1 dessertspoon light soy sauce or a piece of crushed fresh peeled ginger, or a dash of chilli sauce (eg Tabasco).

HOME-DRIED TOMATOES

As I use sun-dried tomatoes in oil quite a lot as a flavouring ingredient, I thought it would be useful to give you a recipe for making something like it yourself at home. They are particularly delicious on pizzas.

Total calories: 200
Saturated fat: Low
Total fat: Low
Protein: Trace
Carbohydrate: High
Cholesterol: Nil
Vitamins: A, C, E
Minerals: Potassium

900 g / 2 lb ripe plum tomatoes
1 dsp olive oil
salt
2 or 3 pinches of oregano

Preheat the oven to 150°C / 300°F / gas2 and lightly grease some baking trays with the oil.

Cut the tomatoes in quarters and remove the pith and seeds.

Arrange the tomato quarters hollow side up on the baking sheets, sprinkle with oregano and put in the oven for about 50 minutes to 1 hour until quite dry.

Allow to cool and use as they are, or store in a jar of olive oil.

Index

Page numbers in *italic* refer to the photographs

Index

CONVERSION CHART

For most general purposes the term 'calorie' is used for the kilocalorie and this is the practice used throughout this book

CALORIES (kcal)	KILOJOULES (kJ)
1	4.18
50	210
100	420
150	630
200	835
250	1,045
300	1,255
400	1,670
500	2,090
600	2,510
750	3,135
1,000	4,180
1,100	4,560
1,200	5,015
1,300	5,435
1,400	5,850
1,500	6,270
1,600	6,690
1,700	7,105
1,800	7,525
1,900	7,940
2,000	8,360
2,100	8,780
2,250	9,405
2,500	10,450

HEIGHT / WEIGHT CHART FOR WOMEN

HEIGHT	AVERAGE WEIGHT	ACCEPTABLE WEIGHT RANGE
4 ft 11 in	104 lb	94–122 lb
1.50 m	47.25 kg	42.75–55.5 kg
5 ft 0 in	107 lb	96–125 lb
1.525 m	48.75 kg	44–57 kg
5 ft 1 in	110 lb	99–128 lb
1.55 m	50 kg	45–58 kg
5 ft 2 in	113 lb	102–131 lb
1.575 m	51.5 kg	46.5–59.5 kg
5 ft 3 in	116 lb	105–134 lb
1.60 m	52.75 kg	47.75–61 kg
5 ft 4 in	120 lb	108–138 lb
1.625 m	54.5 kg	49–62.75 kg
5 ft 5 in	123 lb	111–142 lb
1.65 m	56 kg	50.5–64.5 kg
5 ft 6 in	128 lb	114–146 lb
1.675 m	58 kg	52–66 kg
5 ft 7 in	132 lb	118–150 lb
1.705 m	60 kg	54–68 kg
5 ft 8 in	136 lb	122–154 lb
1.73 m	61 kg	55.5–70 kg
5 ft 9 in	140 lb	126–158 lb
1.755 m	63.5 kg	57–72 kg
5 ft 10 in	144 lb	130–163 lb
1.78 m	65.6 kg	59–74 kg
5 ft 11 in	148 lb	134–168 lb
1.805 m	67 kg	61–76 kg

HEIGHT / WEIGHT CHART FOR MEN

HEIGHT	AVERAGE WEIGHT	ACCEPTABLE WEIGHT RANGE
5 ft 4 in	130 lb	118–148 lb
1.625 m	59 kg	53.5–67 kg
5 ft 5 in	133 lb	121–152 lb
1.65 m	60.5 kg	55–69 kg
5 ft 6 in	136 lb	124–156 lb
1.675 m	62 kg	56.5–71 kg
5 ft 7 in	140 lb	128–161 lb
1.705 m	63.5 kg	58–73 kg
5 ft 8 in	145 lb	132–166 lb
1.73 m	66 kg	60–75.5 kg
5 ft 9 in	149 lb	136–170 lb
1.755 m	68 kg	62–77 kg
5 ft 10 in	153 lb	140–174 lb
1.78 m	69.5 kg	63.5–79 kg
5 ft 11 in	158 lb	144–179 lb
1.805 m	72 kg	65.5–81 kg
6 ft 0 in	162 lb	148–184 lb
1.83 m	73.5 kg	67–84 kg
6 ft 1 in	166 lb	152–189 lb
1.855 m	75.5 kg	69–86 kg
6 ft 2 in	171 lb	156–194 lb
1.88 m	78 kg	71–88 kg
6 ft 3 in	176 lb	160–199 lb
1.905 m	80 kg	73–90 kg
6 ft 4 in	181 lb	164–204 lb
1.93 m	82 kg	75–93 kg